Lord JESUS CHRIST,

you pray for those

who crucify you

and crucify those

who love you.

FATHER JOSEPH DE SAINTE MARIE, OCD

(Domenique Salleron 1931-1984)

PADRE DOMENICO DA CESE, Capuchin
AN ILLUSTRATED BIOGRAPHY

SR. PETRA-MARIA STEINER

VITA COMMUNIS

In memory of Franco di Lorenzo.

Translated

from the Italian Version

by Stella Raimondi and Tamara Klapatch

Copyright © 2018 Vita Communis - Mary, Mother of the Holy Family.
Ossweiler Weg 45, 71334 Waiblingen
Editor: Sr. Petra-Maria Steiner, Dirk Weisbrod
Printed in Germany
Title of the original German version:
Pater Domenico da Cese, OFMCap - Ein Leben in Bildern
www.vitacommunis.de

English version printed in the United States by permission (2019).
Edited by Tamara Klapatch and Mary Jo Loboda.

ISBN: 978-1-7338762-0-9

The Priestly Fraternity of Saint Peter
450 Venard Road
South Abington Township, PA 18411
www.fraternitypublications.com

Above: Father Domenico in the sacristy of the Basilica of Manoppello.

INDEX

Pio of Pietrelcina and Domenico of the Holy Face: two fathers, two brothers from a land of saints.

preface by Paul Badde

Just today, 50 years after the death of the great Padre Pio of Pietrelcina, we realize he had a spiritual brother, not less important but more hidden, to whom a day before his death, the 22nd of September 1968, had passed the baton of sanctity. We're talking about Domenico da Cese who, ten years later, in Turin, reached him in paradise.

Padre Pio was a giant. The amount of his miracles is enormous, just like his inexplicable healings. His stigmata, his bilocation, the clarity with which he read in people's souls and the efficacy of his prayers that are testified by countless individuals. He was frequently humiliated and subjected by his brothers and part of the ecclesiastical powers and this so called "Invidia clericalis" – the common envy between clerics – didn't play a secondary role. As a matter of fact, during his life Padre Pio was already in the fragrance of holiness, so many worshippers took part in his confessional.

Everything we said can also be referred to Padre Domenico da Cese too, whose charity, as already said, occurred in a more discreet way, almost privately. Just now his charity is coming to light in his greatness, like in this new and essential documentation – composed by many pictures and original documents – that Sister Petra-Maria Steiner, from Congregation "Vita Communis - Mary, Mother of the Holy Family" put together with dedication, zeal and attention. In 2010 Sister Petra-Maria moved to Manoppello, in the Sanctuary of Holy Face; she was, just like Sister Blandina Schlömer before her, on the trail of Padre Domenico da Cese, without having the whole matter completely clear.

She became aware of Padre Domenico's monumental, or, even better, miraculous work. He, in addition to all the miracles with which Padre Pio made history, had been able to draw back the attention of the world and the history of the hidden face of God impressed in Christ's sudarium after centuries into the oblivion.

It is, therefore, more than a mere supposition that Padre Domenico could be an incredible saint for the church, along with the great miracle worker from San Giovanni Rotondo.

To Padre Domenico we also owe, and to those few who remember the miraculous healings of Padre Pio, an authentic divine vision to which he got us close in the last 12 years of his indefatigable apostolate. It's the awareness that the Creator of heaven and earth incarnated the human aspect in Jesus of Nazareth, a face of whom we have an incomparable visual documentation in the Christ's sudarium, more convincing than any other text. Padre Domenico was the first one to discover it in Manoppello. Combined with a few cosmic occurrences, such as a 7-magnitude earthquake, we need to mention right from the beginning.

It was the 13th of January of 1915, when at 7:53 a.m. there were four earthquakes that in only five seconds destroyed the city of Avezzano, in Abruzzi, and 15 towns close by; they damaged other towns and caused more than 30,000 victims. Among the villages destroyed there was also Cese dei Marsi. In the Petracca's family, the sisters Laura and Elisa died while the brother Emidio, who went with his father to the morning Mass, remained buried under the ruins of the church and was saved many hours later.

Emidio Petracca became later on – when he entered the Capuchin order in the 1920s – Domenico da Cese. At the moment of the earthquake, the boy was just ten years old; his parents baptized him as Emidio, in honor of Saint

Emidio of Ascoli, a saint bishop and martyr of the IV century, who is considered the protector of earthquakes. After a few hours, an unknown person helped the boy out of the ruins of the collapsed church.

The earthquakes also damaged the Church of Saint Michael, located about 95 km away, on the Tarigni hill, close to Manoppello, where since 1638 was preserved the sudarium of Christ – well protected in a safe with three locks, in a lateral chapel – which was displayed only two times per year to be shown to the believers. In 1923, Father Roberto of Manoppello, who was in those years the guardian of the Convent of the Holy Face, requested some restoration work of the Church of Saint Michael and thought about moving permanently the sudarium from the safe to a new reliquary made of marble, between two sheets of crystal, put on top of the main altar. Since then it's now possible to observe the holy relics closely, which was not feasible for the past 1,870 years, since Mary, the Mother of God, prayed in front of it every evening, tearful, before sleep. *

Without this new display, Domenico da Cese would have never come across the Holy Face, and never recognized him as the man who had rescued him 50 years earlier from the ruins of the collapsed church in Cese, some fifty years earlier. In 1966 in fact, his superiors transferred him, against his will, from Caramanico to Manoppello.

He was 60. And, since that day, he let the Holy Face overwhelm him, just like someone that all of a sudden is struck by lightning by the last and greatest love of his life. He used to get up at 4 a.m. to kneel down and pray in front of the Holy Face. A look was enough to understand that the fabric was different from the others he knew, and it reminded him of a "spider's web." Every day he told the pilgrims that veil was the one laid on Jesus' face in the tomb, just like John writes in his Gospel. He spent countless hours venerating the Holy Face, having better knowledge than all the people in the Early Church, all the fathers in the Church and all the Popes put together. He observed and studied the Veil for so long, which no one else ever did like him since the times of Mary and John. Thanks to Domenico da Cese, we know more about this veil today than ever in history.

In 1977, at the National Eucharistic Congress held in Pescara – to which participated Pope Paul VI as well – Domenico organized an exhibit about the "Holy Face," with an amazing picture that was supposed to let people know about the sudarium for the first time outside Manoppello. Initially though, almost nobody paid any attention to his discovery – contrary to what would happen a year later at the display of the Holy Shroud in the Turin Cathedral, where the Holy Shroud, for the first time in 45 years, was exposed publicly to be venerated by the worshippers. From the 27th of August to the 8th of October of 1978, an endless line of three million of devoted thronged in front of the Cathedral's right gate. Domenico da Cese absolutely wanted to join this line.

For twelve years he advocated the existence of an authentic Christ's icon in the sudarium of Manoppello which corresponded to the Face of the Holy Shroud in Turin. He kept on repeating that both cloths showed the Lord in both images, and now he wanted, or better, had to kneel in front of the Shroud in Turin. In the morning of the 12th of September 1978, around 11 a.m., Padre Domenico, for the first time in his life, stopped in front of the burial shroud with the image of his Lord crucified. When, at the ring of the bell, he had to proceed with the others, he was deeply touched.

The night of the same day, right before 8 p.m., crossing a road, just a meter from the sidewalk, he was hit by a Fiat 500. He was taken to the hospital and died five days later after being in a great deal of pain, surrounded by the people close to him. In this volume Sister Petra-Maria documented Padre Domenico's last days alive in a really impressive way.

Two days later, on the 19th of September, in the Abruzzese edition of "Messaggero" daily paper appeared an obituary notice titled "Mystic monk dies under a car." In the Abruzzi, Padre Domenico was already considered a saint even during his lifetime.

Only today, years later, we understand that, even before the sarcophagus with his body was sealed, his life was transformed, according to the script of God, into a seed that only when it is sown underground would bear fruit. Precisely in those days in-deed, a popular reporter from Verona, Renzo Allegri, travelled to Manoppello, given that the year before he heard a lot of talking about the mysterious Holy Face in the exhibit of Padre Domenico in the Eucharistic Congress in Pescara. Allegri had already written several articles about the display of the Holy Shroud in Turin, and he was interested in viewing the "Holy Face."

However, there wasn't Padre Domenico anymore guiding the visitor and the pilgrims through the history of the sudarium. It was the responsibility of Padre Luciano Antonelli, who was the guardian friar at that moment, telling the reporter what he heard Padre Domenico say a lot of times.

Allegri's article about his visit to Manoppello was published on the 30th of September 1978 on the pages 62-64 in the GENTE, one of the most popular magazines in Italy, titled "A small Shroud in the Abruzzi – It is the Holy Face of Manoppello" and it began like: "The image of Jesus' Face, venerated for almost 500 years in this town in the Abruzzi, is a relic that is enormously valuable. We are talking about a mysterious image impressed on an extraordinarily thin veil called by tradition "the sudarium of Christ." This means it is supposed to be that thin linen tissue that the Mother of Jesus, according to an ancient tradition, laid onto her Son's face before wrapping Him up in the funeral sheet for His burial. Onto this cloth is said to be impressed, in a miraculous way, Christ's face, similarly to what happened for the Shroud in Turin. It is not the same thing we can observe in the Shroud; it is the face of a living person, with his eyes opened and resealed scars: it looks like the image of the Risen Christ ... something inexplicable from a human point of view." It was, in fact, what we can still say today about the sacred veil of Manoppello. It was the spiritual testament of Padre Domenico.

It was like a breach in those dramatic days in that inauspicious year, 1978, which went down in history as the year of the three popes. It's been 40 years! Paul VI died on August 6th; his successor, John Paul I, died only six weeks after his election, on September 28th, 11 days after Padre Domenico's death and two days before the publication of the article on GENTE. One of the days before his departure to Turin, Renzo Allegri must have seen the Holy Face in Manoppello. When Karol Woityla, who was the first pope from a faraway country in Eastern Europe, on the 16th of October looked out the window of Saint Peter's loggia, the seed started to bear his first fruits.

A little later the new Pope exclaimed: "Don't be afraid!" in Saint Peter's Square to a world still divided between east and west: "Open, or rather, throw open your doors to Christ!" It was the sound of fanfare from Rome that made the Soviet Union shake, together with the slow and strenuous beginning of the march of Christ Face starting from the Abruzzi and going slowly towards conquering the world.

Allegri's article must have been one of the few that readers didn't immediately throw away; on October 11th it was published in German in the November edition of the newspaper "DAS ZEICHEN MARIENS" of St. Gallen in Switzerland.

The following winter, the article reached the convent of the Trappist Sisters of Mary Friede close to Cologne and was read by Sister Blandina Paschalis Schlömer. It was like the stone of the tomb of Christ had been removed another time. The one who removed the stone this time was Padre Domenico. Since then, Sister Blandina continued the work she started and kept on affirming that the Shroud in Turin and the Holy Face showed the same person. Despite her superior Sister Fabiana ordered to maintain absolute silence since they entered the convent, this discovery was so extraordinary that Sister Blandina couldn't keep it for herself. A voice inside her told her she had to talk about it and she did with Professor Heinrich Pfeiffer, Professor Werner Buist and eventually to me too: she would tell about everything she learned through mysterious ways from Padre Domenico.

On September 1, 2006, Pope Benedict XVI was the first Pope in four centuries, pausing in prayer in front of the sudarium in Manoppello, silent and astonished; but at the end it was still the humble Padre Domenico da Cese who opened the door of the church and of this exceptional historical moment to the "Mozart of theology" who was sitting on the papal throne.

That day a new chapter in the history of the Holy Face was opened; since that day the Holy Veil draws the attention of both believers and researchers. The rest is already history. The number of pilgrims from all over the world that Domenico da Cese brings to Manoppello increases year after year. No other seed would have brought more fruits.

On October 11, 2013, the Archbishop Bruno Forte declared, in the cathedral of San Giustino, the process of beatification of Padre Domenico officially opened. The last obstacle to the opening of the canonization process was to get the green light from the Turin diocese, given that Domenico died in Turin, which is symbolical.

All this, and even more, tells the documentation that Sister Petra-Maria Steiner presents in this volume: a documentation rich in pictures and in unpublished texts, like testimonies on the life of Padre Domenico. Many people already consider him a saint, the saint of the images of Christ not made by human hands, the Shroud of Turin and Manoppello.

In this volume a great number of well documented miracles can also be found, obtained thanks to his intercession. So, I like to conclude this preface saying: "Dear Padre Domenico of the Holy Face, pray for us!"

Paul Badde

On August 14, 2018, day of the liturgical memory of Saint Maximilian Maria Kolbe, Basilica of the Holy Face of Manoppello

Personal belief of Paul Badde

ACKNOWLEDGEMENTS

This volume is the proof that nothing is impossible for God!

My gratitude is in the first place for Father Domenico da Cese, who relied all his life on God's hands. This book would not exist if it wasn't for his total dedication to the Father. Special thanks go to Father Carmine Cucinelli, to Father Eugenio Di Giamberardino and to Mr. Antonio Bini, who trusted me and made Father Domenico's documents available to me. They encouraged me to write this book since I learned how to know the Father.

A very precious help came from Dr. Dirk Weisbrod. His effort, his culture and his expertise transformed my manuscript into a book. I express my sincere thanks to you from the bottom of my heart.

With gratitude, I can't leave out, Ms. Stella Raimondi and Ms. Tamara Klapatch, who translated this text to English and Angelo and Agatha Rytz. Without them, the English version wouldn't have been realized.

I also thank Rene Udwari for his research work on documents about Padre Domenico.

My sincere gratitude goes also to each and every one who granted me the copyright over the photographs – particularly to Paul Badde, who wrote the preface too. In particular, I would like to mention Franco Di Lorenzo, whom assured to support me but, sadly, shortly after passed away. To him, I dedicate this volume. It was such a delight when Caterina Petracca, his wife, gave me permission to use the pictures he owned!

Lastly, a thanks to everyone who helped me in different ways: praying, but also concretely correcting and adding parts, and travelling to Father Domenico's places.

To the cited ones and to the ones not explicitly mentioned I just would like to say this:

May remain by your side Father Domenico's benediction, which he used to give to his friends, near and far, every night at 8:30. May God recognize your efforts!

Sister Petra-Maria

On August 15, 2018, Feast of the Assumption into Heaven of the Blessed Virgin Mary.

In the small town of Cese, close to Avezzano, in the Apennine regions of the Abruzzi, was born, in 1872, Giovanni Petracca. In 1900, he got married to Caterina Tucceri. But the marriage would be childless for five years.

The husband emigrated temporarily to Argentina to escape poverty, working in stone quarries and earning money to buy a piece of land and a cow.

Thanks to their prayers to the Virgin Mary a son was given to them, born on May 27, 1905: to the future Padre Domenico from Cese, the parents gave the name Emidio Petracca.

At the age of four, young Emidio suffered from infantile paralysis and he wasn't able to walk anymore. In the Petracca's home there were therefore lots of problems: who would have carried on the work of the fields if the son could not walk?

The mother didn't know what to do anymore. So, one day she took him to the church, she put him on the altar of the Virgin Mary and returned him to the Mother of our Lord: from Him the parents received the son as a gift and to Him they gave him back, feeling that he was useless.

The Mother of all mothers looked at the child, listened to the prayer and wiped away the tears of the mother: the little Emidio started moving his feet and legs....

Mary, Mother of God remained the special mother of Emidio. She was always at his side, from the beginning of his life until his death.

The church of Cese before the earthquake of 1915.

The altar of the church of Cese. However, it is uncertain whether it was taken before or after the reconstruction of the church.

3

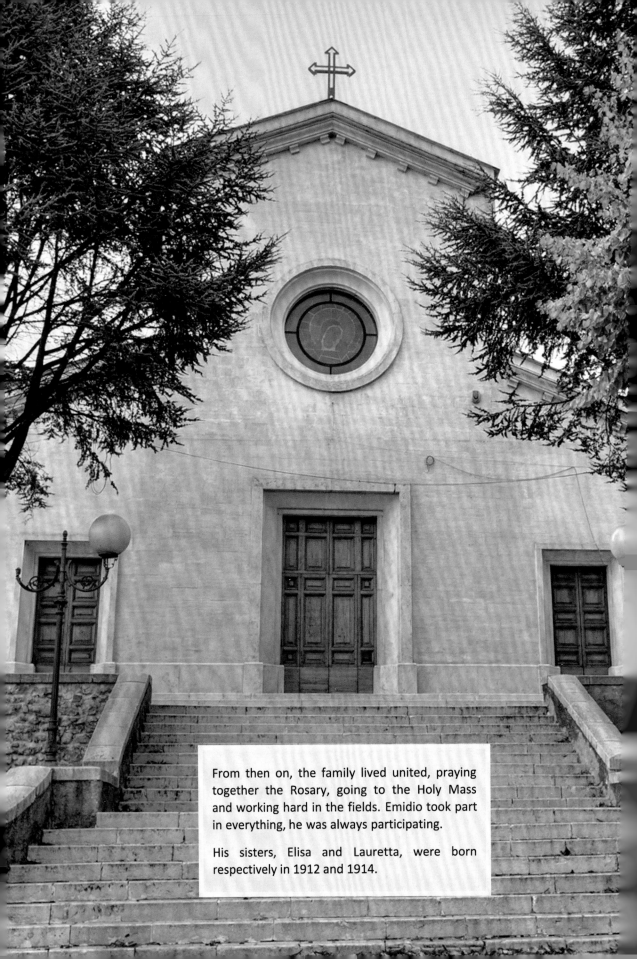

From then on, the family lived united, praying together the Rosary, going to the Holy Mass and working hard in the fields. Emidio took part in everything, he was always participating.

His sisters, Elisa and Lauretta, were born respectively in 1912 and 1914.

The early morning of Wednesday, January 13, 1915, the territory of Avezzano was shocked by a terrible earthquake measuring 7.0 on the Richter Scale.

It lasted a few seconds. However, the damages were of catastrophic proportions: in the whole region over 30,000 people died and more than 15 towns in the Abruzzi completely swept away, razed, including Cese, Emidio's birth town.

If only the inhabitants had listened to what 10-year-old Emidio predicted the day before – he talked about an earthquake that would occur the next night – they could have gotten ready. Anyway, who could have thought a kid was in close contact with God and that the Lord would tell him things that would actually happen in the future?!

The Petracca's house was completely destroyed from the earthquake too. His two younger sisters, Elisa and Lauretta, were buried under the ruins of the paternal home; they did not survive the catastrophe.

The mother was spared by a wedged beam. Emidio and his father at that moment were in the church, to participate in the first mass. They remained buried there until a stranger freed them. This stranger had, later on, a really precious importance for Emidio.

After the earthquake, the house was rebuilt and young Emidio lived there with his father and his mother.

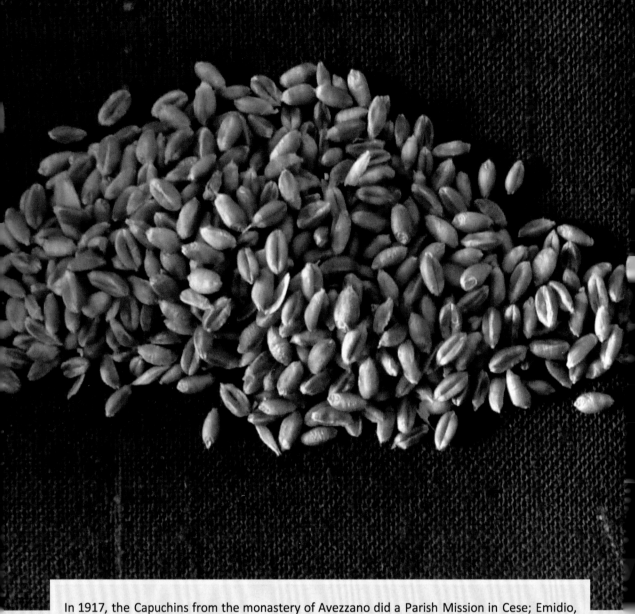

In 1917, the Capuchins from the monastery of Avezzano did a Parish Mission in Cese; Emidio, who was 12 years old, was so moved that he wanted to become a Capuchin too. But he kept this a secret for many years. When, at the end, he decided to ask permission from his dad, he obtained a clear rejection. His father was absolutely against it. Sometime later he came back to his request, asking again for his permission and the answer was a good slap with the prohibition to talk about it again, since Emidio would one day become heir of the land.

So, the barn became Emidio's refuge to pray. While he was praying, the Lord confided to him that his parents would have more children that would take his place and that, given this promise of God, he would have to ask for the permission to enter the convent again. The father indeed allowed him to embrace the religious life, but only after the grain harvest.

That became the motto of his life: He should sow, but another would harvest; he had to become the seed, which is sown first, but has to die for his life to bear rich fruits.

The moment of separation arrived. For his mother (on the left) it was a suffering and at the same time a delight.

After the "yes" from the father, the parents were blessed by the birth of three more children: Elisa, Mario and Angelo.

On November 3, 1921, the father himself took his son Emidio to Avezzano, to the Convent of Saint Francis of Assisi.

At the moment of entry in the convent he was just 16 years old.

He stayed there only a few weeks because he had to complete his school studies.

.

One the 14th of November 1921, his father took him to Vasto, so that he could complete in one single year the fourth and fifth grades of the gym classes there.

It was a big challenge that could only have been overcome by a boy gifted with a firm faith, strengthened by prayers, trusting that God never asks for things bigger than our strengths.

He would become a new plant in the Lord's garden, a plant watered by the sea of his love.

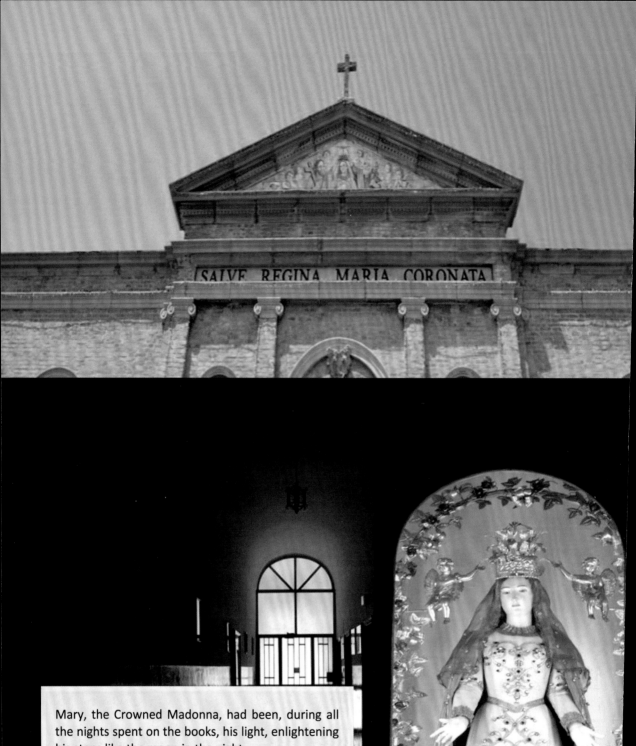

SALVE REGINA MARIA CORONATA

Mary, the Crowned Madonna, had been, during all the nights spent on the books, his light, enlightening his steps like the moon in the night.

Step by step he had been able to sense the next move which would bring him closer to the goal.

The Mother of God, the Crowned Madonna Protectress of Vasto, the mother so loved by him, Mary, was always next to him with Her help. In this way Domenico was able to end his school time and leave Vasto in 1922 to start the novitiate to which he really yearned for.

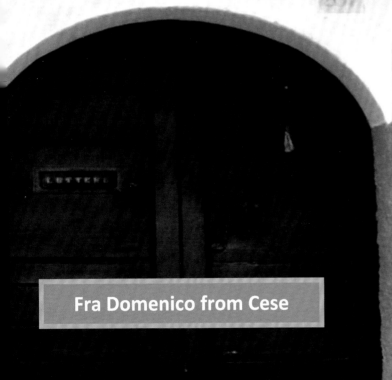

Fra Domenico from Cese

Entering the novitiate, Emidio chose – as by tradition in the Capuchins – the name Fra Domenico.

13

In September 1922, he finally started the definitive separation from his family, his town and his school, so that he could completely give himself to God, to let himself be molded by the religious life and by the following of Christ, based on Saint Francis' spirituality: the love of Christ that cancels, goes beyond and ennobles all the rest, living in the total poverty of the Capuchins.

It's all about training eyes and heart to only address God, to learn how to focus – and to love – humans and the world. Because of this he picked the name "Fra Domenico from Cese". Saint Domenico was a friend of Saint Francis and since then Fra Domenico wanted to live his life in a really radical way.

In all circumstances, in Penne it kept on becoming clearer to him that:

the spiritual journey is about abandoning ourselves,

to allow ourselves to be pierced,

a dying to understand the fullness of Easter.

Becoming rich

in the divine life of Jesus Christ,

hand in hand with Mary

and Saint Francis.

All of them – Jesus, Mary and Saint Francis – suffered the wounds for the salvation of those who accept the Word of God.

With this awareness, in the year 1925, he made his temporary profession.

Fra Domenico from Cese

In the Church, who is being called to build, has to build himself first. Because of this, Fr. Domenico had to move to L'Aquila to start the studies of philosophy and theology.

He stayed there from September 1923 to 1925; at the time he was just 20 years old.

L'Aquila means "the eagle" and already that said it all.

Yes, Padre Domenico had to learn how to fly like just a few do in their path of prayer.

The reason is not just in the fact that each of us has his own vocation but also to the fact that only very few let themselves totally expropriate by God.

His study was prayer and his prayer was study. His soul was so happy for receiving so much spiritual food!

It was far from a mushy sentimentalism, it was about training the will and obedience up to extreme consequences to let God work through his superiors.

Of course, he was obedient when his supervisor interrupted his studies to be trained as a paramedic during his military service in Florence.

Florence, 1925-1927

The love does not withdraw
in front of any sacrifice
since it purifies itself
and grows till it
becomes pure love!

The young Fra Domenico was looking for God. By reciting the Rosary he found the way to be immersed in God. He grew spiritually thanks to his radicalism. And in his radicalism, looked forward to the detachment from himself.

What a very mature thing!

Padre Agostino testifies that in the period spent in Florence: *"he prayed a lot, helped in the house, he was humble and he practiced love of his neighbor."*

In July 1925 – four months later – Fra Domenico returned to Cese for a while, physically exhausted because of the military service. The doctor prescribed to him complete rest.

Jesus and Mary donated everything; he wanted to donate everything too.

After his rest period he went back to Florence until the end of his military service.

The secretary of the Provincial of the Capuchin of Florence testified the 18-month period of military service:

"... the soldier Petracca Emidio – his monastic name is Fra Domenico from Cese – during the military service in Florence always had an appropriate behavior, actually exemplary, from the civil, moral and religious viewpoints. Every time he could, in the convent of Montughi, he took part in the monastic life. He also began the higher studies helped by some fathers."

As his letters show, Padre Domenico always wrote thickly, from a paper margin to the other. This gives an idea of his life: wherever he was, his dedication to God, therefore to his neighbor, was total.

The more assignments the Lord gave him, the more he wanted to have… and the more he had, the more God gave him. Love wants to give! Every sacrifice was a gift of the love to Jesus and Mary and, through them, to his neighbor. Throughout sickness and other suffering, God held him to His heart. Every grace was prepared by the cross.

Suffering was a constant companion in Padre Domenico's life; he would take it and kiss the hand of his heavenly Father, whom gave the cross to him because he knew that:

God is love!

"From the cradle to the grave" – Padre Domenico proceeded through his life hand in hand with Mary – the mother of his heart. With Her by his side he felt protected against inner and outer attacks.

So, in the garden of L'Aquila, he never passed the statue of Mary without greeting Her by reciting a "Hail Mary."

His ailing health was for him, for his whole life, one of the heaviest crosses: he often had high fevers and felt very weak. Despite his physical limits he never backed down from helping.

In Vasto, after the military service, he had to recover his strength. Therefore, he stayed there a while and then he went back to L'Aquila.

The holy Mother of God added to his cross a "sweet" surprise. The Rosary itself had to become a chain to him: with every decade of the Rosary he became more attached to the Mother of Jesus – Mother and Son! As a gift for a loyal and absolute love like the one of a child she redirected his life towards the total dedication; she wanted to help him become more and more similar to Her beloved Son, to Jesus Christ.

April 8, 1928 was the day of the perpetual profession that Fra Domenico released in L'Aquila.

The day before he himself wrote the text of the perpetual profession and the day after he wrote underneath:

"I, Fra Domenico from Cese, Capuchin friar, once called Emidio Petracca, son of Giovanni and Caterina Tucceri, completed my religious education and three years of temporary profession; I also turned 23 years old. I was born on March 28, 1905. I pled repeatedly the Provincial Father to deliver my religious vows freely, of my own will, this morning at 8:00, on the day, month and year indicated above, in the hands of aforesaid Provincial and the entire religious family, according to the rules in force in the Order. And in this truth, I wrote and signed this letter in my own hand. Fra Domenico from Cese Capp.

Fra Roberto da Manoppello Min. Prov.

Fra Serafino di Tussio, Witness   Fra Andrea dal Tufo Capp., Witness."

To him it was not something superficial. Inside of him burned the fire of love grown through suffering. Obedience is strenuous if one is not aware he's being guided always and only by God, our Father. Just a childlike soul can remain obedient in every circumstance of life. Fra Domenico had the candor of a child. Because of this, with inner joy and strong determination, he could put his hands in the Provincial Father's, promising to live the endless love in virginity, the real freedom in obedience and the absolute trust in poverty.

When the Provincial Father told him, he would be transferred to Sulmona, Fra Domenico told him he felt too weak. *"But"* – he wrote – *"In obedience I'll go wherever you want and I respectfully kiss your hands."* The convent of Saint Francis of Paola in Sulmona became his new house.

From each step of obedience, even though against himself and his physical condition, arose graces thousands of times greater. Domenico had to first receive the diaconate and then the priestly ordination. But until that happened, once again his trust was checked.

In preparation for the priestly ordination, the correctness of his perpetual profession was called into question. To remove all doubts, he was obligated to repeat it on October 1, 1931, so that he could be consecrated a priest.

NICOLAUS IEZZONI
EPISCOPUS   A.D. 1907

Yes, God turned everything towards good through the intercession of Mary: in the Cathedral of Sulmona, on the day of the feast of the Divine Motherhood of Mary, October 11, 1931, Domenico received the priestly ordination from the Bishop Nicola Iezzoni.

Just like the prelude of the pipe organ initiates the Holy Mass, the priestly ordination initiates the most important phase of Padre Domenico's life. But sitting at the pipe organ was not him (like in the picture) but rather the Holy Spirit. With the ordination, he was associated to the redemption work of Jesus Christ becoming with Him a sacrificial offering and together grace – and the Holy Spirit set the pace.

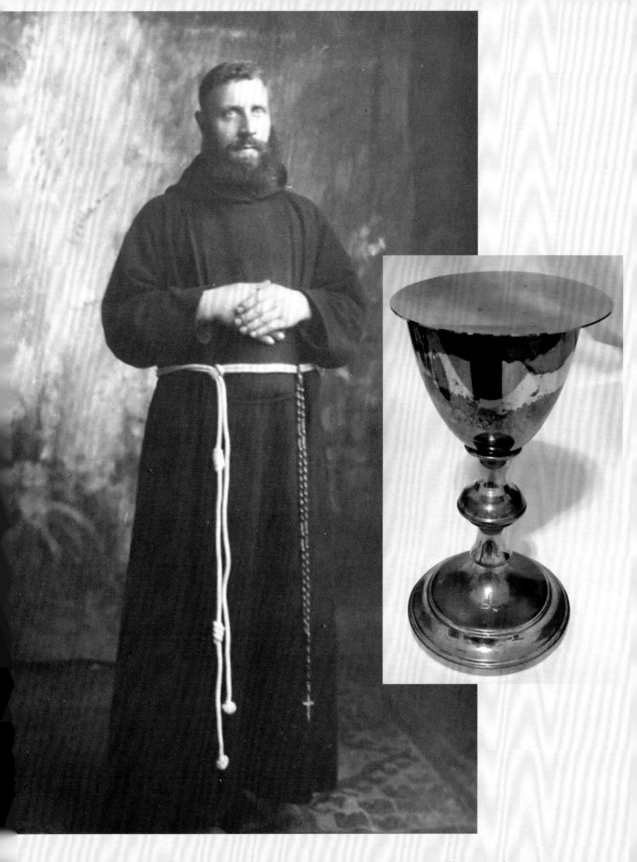

Padre Domenico knew what being a priest of Jesus Christ meant: let yourself be transformed, shaped by the will of the Father, to become in Him like bread that can be received by the people and the world – for the salvation of the souls, in honor of God, one and triune. He felt so happy when, since 1933, he could preach and, in the confessions, free the souls from sins!

The young priest went back to L'Aquila to complete his theological studies. He was glad he had more time for studying and praying. But now it was different since he glimpsed the dark clouds from the north thickening over the country. He completed his studies and then became a hospital chaplain in L'Aquila.

Under the title "Mary, the everlasting help," He venerated a lot the Mother of God. He knew that she always supported him and who relied on Her.

n November 27, 1939, the day of the Feast of the Miraculous Medal of Rue du Bac, Padre Domenico
btained the travel document which allowed him to carry out the religious duties out of the military service.
ne Second World War had already started.

ne picture of his passport already showed a strong personality of a priest who drew his strength from
orship. As if he had foretold what would have struck Europe in the following years. On October 3, 1940 he
as called to arms and sent to Trieste.

Visit to Padre Pio, 1940

Before leaving to go to the front, Padre Domenico wanted to go to San Giovanni Rotondo to visit Padre Pio; he stayed there from the 19th to the 23rd of November 1940.

When he saw him, Padre Pio exclaimed: *"Finally I have the honor to see a military chaplain with the cassock."*

Both of them were well aware that the Second World War was much more than a war of politicians hungry for power; it was a war for the dominion of God over the world.

Padre Pio must have also predicted to Padre Domenico he would not stay for long at the front.

The night of November 23, at 10:30 p.m., he said goodbye to Padre Pio and left for Trieste.

e spent the first months in the Convent of the Capuchins of Montuzza, in Trieste. The 35-year-old Padre omenico, would write once a month to the Provincial in L'Aquila to report his experiences – as far as the ate censorship allowed.

31

Based on the postcards he sent to the Provincial, we can retrace his whereabouts as a soldier:

October 1940: Postumia (Adelsberg) – today in Slovenia

October 29, 1940: Triest

November 20, 1940: reentry in Avezzano

January 15, 1941: arrival in Trieste – 'Sassari Division'

April 12, 1941: Villa del Nevoso – today Bistrica, in Slovenia

April 16, 1941: Čabar, Croatia – for 24 hours

From May 5 to May 31, 1941: Spalato

From June 6, 1941: around Croatia

From June 30, 1941: Dubrovnik

September 1941: Obljaj-Grahovo

From October 1941: Dubrovnik

October 18, 1941: discharge from military service

October 19, 1941: reentry in Avezzano

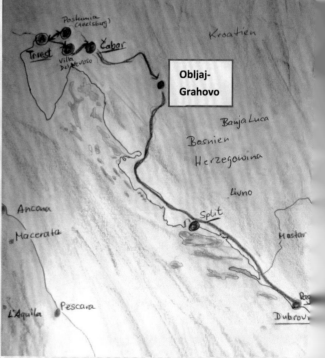

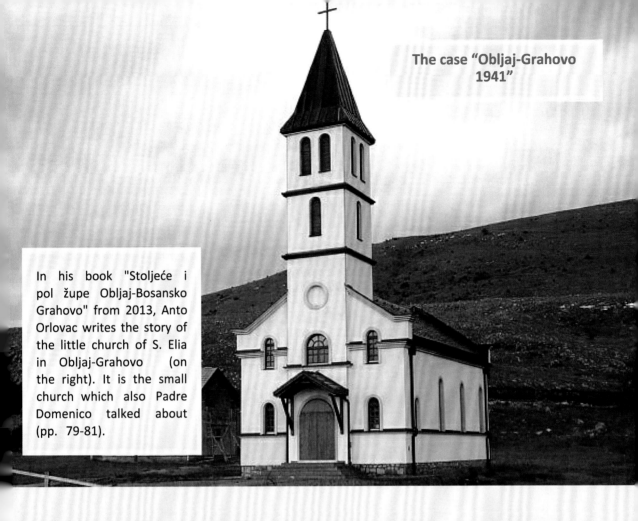

In his book "Stoljeće i pol župe Obljaj-Bosansko Grahovo" from 2013, Anto Orlovac writes the story of the little church of S. Elia in Obljaj-Grahovo (on the right). It is the small church which also Padre Domenico talked about (pp. 79-81).

The young parish priest of the Bosnian village Obljaj-Grahovo, Father Juraj Gospodnetić, was tortured and killed on July 28, 1941 in Grohovo at the age of 31, in a brutal way.

Anto Orlovac, the author, began writing that at the beginning of September 1941, the Italian soldiers, Padre Domenico included, entered this village. Padre Domenico wrote in a letter, without a date on it, to the Bishop of Split (in today's Croatia).

"Now all the sacred objects of the church: cassocks, chalices, patens for the hosts, pyxes have been mostly damaged, stepped on and thrown in a stack of rubble. During my presence here as a military chaplain I learned that here is present the Blessed Sacrament. So, I went to the tabernacle and I opened it; in the pyx I found lots of consecrated Hosts in a paten. I took everything with me and the next day I reordered everything in the church, I only kept the consecrated Hosts in the pyxes. I still have to inform you about the fact that now the church is open, with no keeper and the key is in the lock. Because of this I respectfully plead you to handle this matter as soon as possible. I am sure His Eminence will do whatever is needed. I offer you my heartfelt respect and I remain at Your disposal. Your faithful Petracca Padre Domenico, military chaplain."

GOSPODNETIĆ don Juraj

Er ist am 9. I. 1910. in Postire auf der Insel Brač geboren, im 1938. zu Priester geweiht.

Als Pfarrer in Obljaj-Bosansko Grahovo (Diözese Banja Luka) wurde er dort am 28 Juli 1941 von serbischen Cetniks grausam gemartert und getötet.

Cfr, A. Baković, Hrvatski martirologij XX stoljeća, 1, Svećenici mučenici Crkve u Hrvata, Zagreb 2007, p. 214.

On October 2, 1941 the bishop of Split, Klement Bonefačić (1870-1957, picture on the right) received the letter.

Padre Domenico was entrusted with taking to Knin at the convent of the Franciscans all the religious objects.

On November 6, 1941 the commander wrote that *"he had Padre Domenico take to Knin at the convent of the Franciscan the pyx, the ostensory, the harmonium."*

Padre Domenico added in his own writing: *"...I carried out the assignment given to me."*

The Bishop of Split forwarded Padre Domenico's letter to the Bishop of Banja Luca, Jozo Garić (1870-1946, in the picture), whom, however, received it just on the 10th of October 1941.

Only through it, he understood the martyrdom of the young priest Juraj Gospodnetić, the situation of the place and of the church of Saint Elija.

On the 13th of October 1941 the Bishop Garić wrote to Padre Domenico begging him to do whatever was possible to hand out the sacred objects and the registry of the baptisms to trustful people.

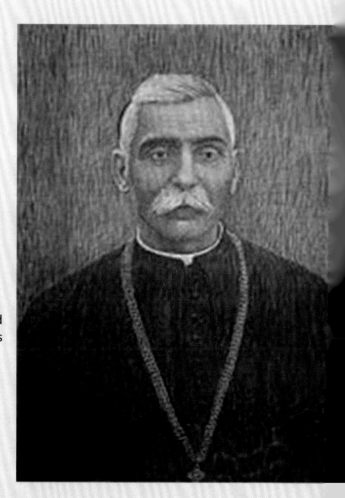

Neither the Bishop of Banja Luca, nor Padre Domenico could be aware that the Military Archbishop in charge, Angelo Bartolomasi, on the 26th of September 1941 sent from Rome a letter to the Provincial of the Abruzzi to dismiss Padre Domenico from the military service.

L'Ordinario Militare
per l'Italia

N° 7105 ¾

Roma 26 settembre 1941 XIX

Al Rev.mo P.Ministro Provinciale dei
Minori Cappuccini – dell'Abbruzzo
                                    L'AQUILA

Vi comunico che in data odierna ho dovuto disporre il ricollocamento in congedo del P.Domenico al secolo PETRACCA Emidio.

Egli é un'ottimo religioso e non vi é nulla a che dire circa la sua condotta sacerdotale, ma non ha saputo ambientarsi nell'ufficio di cappellano militare ed inoltre non sa parlare in pubblico in modo adeguato.

Perciò l'Autorità militare mi ha chiesto la sua sostituzione.

Benedico.

+ Angelo Bartolomasi

ARCIVESCOVO ORDINARIO MILITARE

The translation of the letter reads:

"I want to tell you that today I had to order that Father Domenico born Petracca Emidio is dismissed.

He is an excellent religious and there is nothing to say that disgraces his priestly behavior, however he was not able to adjust himself to the duties of a military chaplain and his public speaking was inappropriate. That's why the military authorities asked me to replace him."

We can only imagine that, for Padre Domenico, the martyrdom of the priest and the situation in Obljaj-Grahovo must have been a huge suffering: it was Jesus Christ, it was the Church that had been dishonored. Saint Francis taught his brothers to consider the church as the house of God and because of this to never neglect it and to always choose the best for it.

Certainly, in the middle of the war, no commander would tell his soldiers to load on a car a harmonium, books and religious objects, to take them from the upland to the level ground, especially towards the direction they came from.

But for Padre Domenico the religious element was above the insanity of the war which only brings pain and suffering in the families and among the population. Therefore, in his eagerness he could demand something that did not seem appropriate to the commander.

The religious authenticity of Padre Domenico struck, but he turned out to be at times unpleasant because of his radicalism and the love for truth which refused even the slightest compromise. However, for him Jesus Christ was above the natural world, not to mention the unnatural element present in every war.

On the 18th of October 1941, one day before leaving Croatia, Padre Domenico wrote to the Provincial the below experience:

"Once, at 4 in the afternoon I went into the office, in Mary's small room, where I pray the Divine Office. Then Mary came back and I told her: 'You know that dogs also eat the crumbs falling from the table of the rich?' Later I left, I took in my hand the crucifix of my Rosary. While I was praying the Rosary, from all the holy wounds of the cross came out warm and bright red blood.

This happened in the presence of Mister Basso and his wife.

The blood of the Crucified poured out of the side and of the whole chest and also of the crown of thorns, forming drops. Watching them, we were moved to tears and we cried. This happened at 5 in the afternoon on the 18th of October 1941. (a lot of people were present).

Signed P. Domenico, capuchin"

On October 19, 1941, it was a Sunday, Padre Domenico was returning to the convent of Avezzano from his service as a war chaplain. He used to write to his Provincial about his poor health condition: *"For over a month I have really high fevers, from 105.8°F to 109.4°F, my legs are really swollen and the feet have open wounds which bleed; I always have strong migraines and on top of that I can't even sleep. When I told these things to the doctor of Dubrovnik, I had permission to be on night watch duty for a week."* And continues: *"On October 8th came a new chaplain in the field of Dubrovnik bringing a letter saying he was the new chaplain. Ten days later I was called back to Trieste. I would really like to go to Padre Pio so that I can restore spiritually. I would like to give to my poor mother the money I received, and she has never received not even a cent from me."*

Agostina Lazzarini, a spiritual daughter of Padre Domenico, reports that he received the stigmata in Croatia. Maybe those are the first signs: headache due to the crown of thorns and bloody feet? Or maybe he meant, *"Bread crumbs fallen from the table"*? We don't know exactly because he himself does not write anything precise about it.

Though the testimony of the soldiers is really fitting: *"You, father, are a person absolutely extraordinary!"*

It is weird he did not refer to his Provincial what happened in Obljaj-Grahovo. But, as a priest and authentic son of Francis, he had just done his duty so, for him, everything was all right.

After the Second World War you would think peace was a precious treasure. But one thing is the external peace, and another is the peace in a community. Due to his radicalism, Padre Domenico always had some brothers who conflicted with him. What these confreres did to him well into the 1960s is unimaginable.

So, he did not want to be transferred from Avezzano for health reasons alone but also did not want to be always "the subject of the scandal." The Provincial however did not want to. The vow of obedience, the love and the patience of Padre Domenico were extremely tested.

The missing comprehension for his radicalism as for the envy – both for his candor and the gift he was provided with – were the reasons why new storms kept happening over him.

God had wanted to leave him in this trial for many years. Since He loved him, he wanted to sacrifice him. His life should have just one sun, Jesus Christ, and just one moon, Mary, who had to light his life.

But with what did he give scandal? He stayed in the church most of the time since he could not sleep and was sick. During confessions people would experiece his spiritual gifts, the care of souls, the ability to direct them and the wisdom that radiated from him. More and more people rushed, even from neighboring towns, and wanted Padre Domenico to confess them or to have his blessing.

The word spread: *"He's not a priest like the others!"*. Adults, children, the elderly – everyone wanted to go to him. Later on, when he was moved elsewhere, the farmers would follow him by foot or with carriages pulled by oxen. Wherever he went lots of people would follow him. In some of his brothers this caused envy. So, they became the "instrument of his sanctity". God agrees only to what is needed for our sanctification.

From this moment on, he dedicated himself totally and completely to the Cross, and the Rosary was always in his hands.

It also strikes the fact that, ever since then, his look was constantly turned upwards, not anymore, as it used to happen, towards the ground.

Like a child he always looked up, towards his Father and his celestial Mother.

This proves his inner freedom.

All for JESUS!

What happened in the period of the great trial under this cross? Here a change seems to have taken place. Padre Domenico wrote:

"Still more suffering, so that more souls can be saved."

In this time, he also wrote an essay titled:

"All for Jesus."

Here he found his inner freedom: the burden of life does not crush but rather gives the life its meaning. The pain, if united with Jesus, saves the souls. This is love! True love loves in sacrifice, often against the person itself.

Maybe today Padre Domenico points his look towards us and asks us:

"Did you grow wiser under your cross

or

did you let it crush you?"

He taught believers to carry their own cross and often he would carry theirs. Or he would show them that they got the cross themselves and suggested the path to live following Christ in God.

The grain of wheat has to die, only then it brings rich fruit. Even if Padre Domenico was still in the dark, the new life has already become visible.

For those who wanted to be sanctified, he was confessor, assistant and for many spiritual children, a father.

Every three years, in September, the Capuchins normally change convents. Of course, there are always some exceptions. Padre Domenico was transferred only in 1946 to Luco dei Marsi.

Here he met the twelve-year-old Maria Venditti that was brought to him by some friends of hers.

Maria Venditti

Until today Maria Venditti from Pescara remains a spiritual daughter of Padre Domenico. After she got married, in 1958, she was expecting her first child but her health conditions were miserable. The doctors were of the opinion that if she didn't have an abortion, she would not survive for longer than a month. In this awful situation she ran to Padre Domenico who was surprised and asked her loudly what she wanted from him. She told him everything through her tears; he reassured her and answered: *"This one will be born and you will stay alive too."* *"This one?"* she asked with astonishment. *"It will be a boy then?!"* *"Yes"* he answered *"It will be a boy and will be born after the 15th of May!"* *"But I really wanted a girl!"* she responded with a certain sadness. *"After a short time you will give birth to a girl too"*, was his response.

Everything happened exactly how Padre Domenico told her: Felice was born on the 27th of May 1958 and the 14th of July 1960, Elisabetta was born. In Campli, Padre Giuseppe Costantini took a picture where you can see Maria, the mother-in-law, Felice and Elisabetta all together with Padre Domenico.

Padre Domenico always remained the counselor and spiritual father of the Venditti's family. One day the parents told him they enrolled Felice in the Salesian School. He was bewildered and asked *"Don't you think the boy should undertake a military career?"* To this day Felice is grateful for the question of Padre Domenico since it was exactly what he wanted: to become a Carabiniere, just like his father.

Here is Maria Venditti today. She treasures the rosary Padre Domenico brought her from the Holy Land, which is in a little box in plain sight on the coffee table.

She can recount other episodes about Padre Domenico.

For instance, the event happened in September 1978: it was the first or second Sunday of the month when she wanted to go back to Manoppello to hear Padre Domenico's mass. The son Felice, who volunteered at the Red Cross, was too tired and didn't go with her. Maria felt bad for it.

Padre Domenico, before or after the mass, all of a sudden said: *"The mother who is now sad because her son didn't come here too, doesn't have to be sad. But she has to know that her son won't see Padre Domenico anymore".* Did he already know the day of his death? Shortly afterwards, indeed, he died.

The night of Padre Domenico's death, Elisabetta, who was 16, dreamt that the Padre fell and was there, on the ground, in his own blood. Completely shaken, she rushed to her mother, she told her about the dream and asked her what it could have meant.

Later on, they found out it was exactly the night in which Padre Domenico died.

When Maria underwent surgery for her eye, in Bologna, in March 1995, some complications occurred since they cut too deeply and the ocular fluid came out.

The eye was bandaged and they decided to have a new surgery on her the next day while other patients, operated like her, could serenely go back home.

She stayed alone in the dark room and she cried for a long time because she was afraid of losing her eyesight.

Then a monk entered the room and asked her: *"Maria, why are you crying?"* She told him the whole situation and he answered: *"I'll pray a lot for you. Don't you cry but instead pray yourself too!"*

The day after they gave her a tranquilizer and brought her to the operating room. A doctor went to her because he wanted to check on the eye once again.

The nurse shoved the bed to the side of the corridor, the doctor removed the bandage from the eye, he looked at it closely and hurried to call the professor on the phone asking him to come there right away; he answered that he did not have time since he was about to start Maria Venditti's operation.

But, considering the insistence of the doctor, he went, observed carefully the eye and said amazed: *"You must have lots of saints in Heaven! You cannot even see a scar here. The eye is healed!"*

Maria Venditti today says: *"The monk who came to me could only be Padre Domenico. He knew my name and I didn't know any other friar!"*

As already happened to Job, God permits sometimes that a person undertakes hard tests. Humanly you could think: that's enough! But the Lord knows what He does.

On June 27, 1947, Padre Domenico was present at the death of his beloved mother, Caterina Tucceri; this was for him a suffering and, at the same time, a comfort.

Just 10 days before, he celebrated a mass for the anniversary of his father Giovanni's death. He did this every year since June 17, 1933, when he celebrated the Funeral Mass for his father.

Now he did the same for his mother, to whom he was really close.

Sometimes, the pain is a blood drop coming out from the heart; it's like "the lily in the fields", or the poppy, more beautiful than Solomon's silk if the soul agrees with God's plans!

From Luco dei Marsi he was sent to build the convent of Trasacco, where he became the guardian. One year later the job was completed.

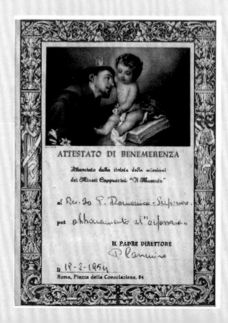

He loved this little convent and the people living in town. On the right you can see a certificate of merit released on February 19, 1954.

Campli, which is part of Teramo's province, is located in a splendid position on a hill. The world there appears to be in order. But right there Padre Domenico had to experience, once again, the cross together with the grace.

For a period of time it was his superior himself to oppose him and the many people who came to him.

But the cross stayed in the background; in the foreground there always was the grace of God that supported him and that he, in turn, donated to the souls. Even Padre Pio, from San Giovanni Rotondo, sent him lots of people and repeated:

"Why do you come to me from the Abruzzi? Go to Padre Domenico, save time and money for the long trip!" And when people asked him: *"But where is this padre?"* he was always able to say precisely where Padre Domenico was in that exact moment.

Padre Domenico was becoming more and more a master capable of uprooting the fear of suffering. He showed to everyone that exists just one door, the one which leads to the union with God and, therefore, he was never tired of referring to the cross.

Filled as he was with the gifts of the Holy Spirit, he knew how to guide man:

- He opened their eyes to recognize the sins through the gift of reading into souls.

- He cured illnesses

- He pointed the path which led to God.

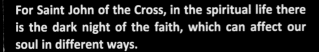

For Saint John of the Cross, in the spiritual life there is the dark night of the faith, which can affect our soul in different ways.

Padre Domenico had already been through a lot of dark nights of the soul: the earthquake of 1915, the illnesses which left him no peace and the envy of his brothers.

To those another one adds up. Some complained to the Provincial about his behavior: according to a priest the penitence given by him after the confession were not appropriate, a bishop sustained that he donated objects which could lead to superstition; a woman complained that he hid her husband in a convent...

But luckily Mary, the Mother of God, enlightens every night!

As already happened in the Second World War, Padre Domenico had sacred ornaments at heart, as a true Saint Francis' follower. Given that in Campli there only were ruined vestments, in bad conditions, he wrote to His Holiness – he was Pope John XXIII – and begged him to send new vestments in all the liturgical colors.

A parishioner of the Church of Santo Spirito in Sassia in Rome confirms the existence of this letter with his stamp and his signature on the back of the page.

The letter though only arrived at the Secretary of State, and not to Pope John XXIII. The response to Padre Domenico arrived through the Bishop of Teramo, in charge of Campli. I'll let you imagine the rest....

To this period dates this testimony of Padre Romeo Carosi:

"The years I spent in Campli (Teramo) with Padre Domenico can be summarized in a few words: I could see with my eyes he was a man of prayer and sacrifice because he would get up at two in the morning to go to the church to pray. His word represented for everyone a real solace and an encouragement. And he always neglected to have dinner to feel mortified".

"JMJF Very Rev. P. Provincial

Padre Domenico thanks you for the great thoughtfulness you showed, the desire of wanting to renew my permission to deprive my dinner meal for my whole life, to the praise and glory of Our Lord Jesus Christ. With deep respect I kiss your sacred right hand and I am yours affectionately.

Yours Padre Domenico"

Translation of a letter he wrote to the Provincial Father.

What Padre Romeo testifies is not a religious temporary exaltation. Padre Domenico actually requested – and obtained – to be relieved of having dinner. This relief was then renewed. This sacrifice was never viewed as such, but he made it in honor of God.

You could see his love from big and small sacrifices he offered to Jesus our Lord, to His honor or for the salvation of souls.

Padre Domenico's place in the choir of Campli's Church.

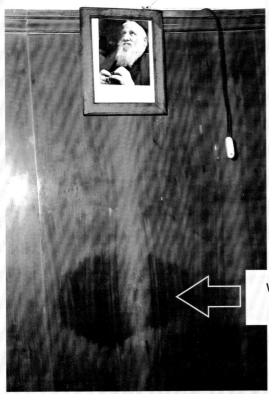

This testifies he prayed continuously, just like he confessed without a break. It was his place, his home! He spent a lot of time sitting in the choir, so much that his sweat impregnated it, modifying the color.

Who knows how much it costed him to take on himself, together with Jesus, people's sins, and then love them, advise them, comfort them about what they needed.

A shepherd based on the heart of Jesus!

Where he laid his shoulders, the wood turned black.

Spot he laid his feet, was discolored (the arrows show their position).

Two things that Padre Domenico had at heart the most: priest's sanctity and the veneration of Mary, the Mother of the Lord. He became a member of two associations that corresponded with this passionate desire.

He knew what it meant when priests did not let themselves be sanctified; therefore, he wanted to pray particularly for them and offer every possible sacrifice for their sanctification. It was clear to him the principle whereby holy priests can accomplish God's will and lead people. For this reason, in 1946, he joined the priest's association "Unio Cleri pro Missionibus in Italia."

Below, his membership card.

Additionally, Padre Domenico had always been a son of Mary and remained such until his death. Who can help us better than Mary, the Mother of Our Lord Jesus Christ?!

Their hearts have always beaten in unison. Didn't Mary promise to S. Catherine Labouré, in 1830, to accomplish miracles to those who wear the Miraculous Medal? How many miracles had already taken place!

Today, more than ever, we need miracles. Because of this, in 1961, he decided to join the Association of the Miraculous Medal: he personally experienced Mary's attentive love, so he recommended this "sweet" instrument granted by God, one and triune.

In the spring of 1964, Padre Domenico went to Penne to the annual spiritual exercises. Padre Gaudenzio da Montenero, who hailed from the convent of Manoppello, went there too. It was exactly Padre Gaudenzio – who later had the hotel called "Casa del Pellegrino" built – the one who took him for the first time in Manoppello, to the Holy Face.

The night of his arrival in Manoppello, the custodian of the convent, Padre Enrico Carusi (picture on the left), accompanied him to see the Holy Face of Jesus.

Padre Domenico stayed silent for a long time in front of the Holy Face, deep in his thoughts.

Bruno Sammaciccia, in his book *"Padre Domenico Capuchin, A great Franciscan spirit"*, reports (pp. 72 and following) that the Padre, in the Holy Face, identified the person whom in 1915, after the earthquake, saved him from the ruins of the church of Cese.

Six months before his 60th birthday, the time came for Padre Domenico to change convents. He was indeed transferred to Caramanico Terme, located in the National Park of Majella, about 650 meters above sea level.

Since XVI century, Caramanico is known as a thermal resort. Lots of people try to alleviate their pains in the sulfurous water, and the thermal baths give the place a particular character. Even today, Capuchins convent rooms host priests and bishops who go there to be cured – They also offer rooms for youth camps.

Here, Padre Domenico started a new phase of his life – a new dawn?

It was not just the locals who were pleased for the new priest's arrival, but also lots of people who hastened to him. The gift of reading the souls allowed Padre Domenico, during the sacrament of confession, to lead the followers towards the path of sanctification. His uninterrupted prayer and his blessing, in some cases, brought also an external recovery, namely of the body.

Since his arrival, he was like a "magnet" attracting people. His task was to reconcile the souls with God and to show them the way to heaven.

He knew this was possible only if he burdened himself with their cross, with the aid of prayer – and he would never back down, aware of the fact that he had to lead every soul to Christ.

His health was more than precarious: he suffered from rheumatoid arthritis (or chronic poly-arthritis, an infection of the limbs), varicose veins, psoriasis and duodenum ulcer, and also the consequences of feet freezing, dating back to the war period.

So, it was prescribed to him the sulfurous water of Caramanico. Padre Domenico was grateful because the therapy was helping.

The greatest support though was from the Holy Mass and the rosary; this way he could also lavish to those asking him for help, the gift of grace.

People would rush to Caramanico from all over Italy and his fame was expanding even further.

In all the years of his priesthood, the sacrament of confession was the key point where to attack Padre Domenico: the accusation was that the encouragement and the penances he assigned were not edifying but destructive. Since Campli, some letters sent to the Provincial Father always went back to the same point, briefly: "calumny and calumny".

On August 22, 1966, the Feast day of The Immaculate Heart of Mary, the Provincial Father wrote a letter to Padre Domenico which had the impact of a stab in his priestly heart: on behalf of the vow of obedience, he was forbidden, from September 1, 1966 to September 15, 1967, to practice the ministry of confession and therefore to reconcile the souls with God.

(here is a part of the document)

> a correzione e penitenza canonica, in virtù di Santa Obbedienza, ORDINIAMO alla P.V. di non ascoltare CONFESSIONI di sorta per nessun motivo, servatis de jure servandis, dal giorno primo di settembre al giorno quindici di settembre prossimo inclusivamente.
>
> Se la P.V. non ottemperasse a quanto ingiunto, incorrerebbe nelle censure.

"I want to know Christ (...) becoming like him in his death" (Phil 3:10)

For Padre Domenico the prohibition was a fatal blow, inflicted by his own superiors. His followers would feel abandoned. But he kept this huge pain to himself!

On September 8, 1966 the father guardian of that time, Padre Giambattista, wrote a letter to the Provincial Father:

"Padre Domenico read and understood your letter. We read and reread it together several times and Padre Domenico felt really, really bad.

For him this was the biggest punishment his superiors ever imposed on him. Padre Domenico suffered for it enormously, both morally and physically (....) but I already — after eight days — pray in the name of real love the most reverend superiors, motivating the prayer with my submission and indignity, to send Padre Domenico a new letter to shorten the time of his profound pain."

He had nothing left, he only had the recourse to trust in God – that is real faith!

The Mother of Our Lord stayed under the cross of Jesus. She was also Padre Domenico's mother and she stayed close to him.

Mary is the Queen of Heaven and Earth; she was able to "sweeten" every cross. Despite the pain and the sense of abandonment, he did not feel alone reciting the rosary, he sensed the support of the closeness of his beloved celestial mother.

Padre Giambattista's letter did not receive an answer. On October 12, 1966 Padre Domenico wrote to the Provincial, in which no mention was made that he may hear confessions again.

We deduce that the prohibition was still effective. In the letter, Padre Domenico reacts to the order of the Provincial who communicated to him the transfer to Manoppello.

The original letter written by him to the Provincial:

Caramanico Terme, 12 Ottobre 1966

Molto Reverendo P. Provinciale,

Vi scrivo poche parole, per farVi presente il mio caso. Con gli ultimi cambiamenti sono stato trasferito al Convento di Manoppello. In tutta la mia vita ho sempre ubbidito e non sono mai stato di motivo di fastidi o disturbi per il rifiuto di ubbidienza. Però ora Vi prego di considerare il mio caso.

Sono ormai vecchio. Il clima di Caramanico i medici l'hanno riscontrato molto buono per me. Io sono malato di " psoriasi " una specie di eczema, alla testa, che mi da tanto prurito e tanto fastidio... e quì nella continua lavanda con acqua solfurea ; acqua che uso molto spesso e in certi periodi anche quotidianamente come bevanda per purificare il sangue, ho trovato un buon rimedio... Per di più quì ho trovato un buon barbiere che ogni due o tre giorni viene in convento e mi passa il rasoio sulla cute della testa, per togliere quella specie di squame che mi produce la psoriasi. Trovare ora altrove un altro barbiere che mi si voglia prestare alla stessa carità, non è certamente troppo facile, anche perchè detta operazione è ripugnante e nauseante, oltre che per me sarebbe non poca umiliazione andare in cerca di un simile aiuto.

Inoltre io ho anche l'ulcera duodenale che la curo anche molto bene con le acque termali che sono in questa zona, che mi fanno molto bene.

Infine ho anche i piedi congelati e per il buon clima locale, specie ne periodo invernale, non ne soffro molto.

In considerazione di questi mali che mi affliggono e che posso provare con certificati e diagnosi mediche, chiedo la carità a voler prendermi in considerazione e voler revocare il mio trasferimento a Manoppello, ed a volermi consentire la permanenza a Caramanico. Penso anche che è la prima volta in vita mia che mi permetto fare una simile richiesta ad un mio Superiore. E Vi chiedo questo a titolo di carità, per me che sono anche vecchio.

Sperando che non mi sarà negata questa carità, Vi bacio la mano e Vi chiedo la benedizione.

P. Domenico da Cese.

Padre Domenico
Pà Cese

Translation of the letter documented on the previous page:

Carmanico Terme, 12 October 1966

Dear Father Provincial,

To remind you of my case, I write a few words to you. By the last order I was transferred to the monastery of Manoppello. I have always obeyed all my life, and I have never been annoyed or disturbed for refusing anything. But please consider my case now.

I am old now. [61 years, Author's Note] The climate of Caramanico the doctors found very good for me. I suffer from "psoriasis," a kind of eczema on the head, that causes me so much itching and discomfort .... and here in the continuous treatment with sulfur water – water, which I use very often and in certain periods daily as a drink, I've found a good remedy .... Besides, I have a good barber who comes to the convent every two or three days and rubs the skin of my head with the razor to remove the dandruff that causes psoriasis. Now finding another barber to treat me out of charity is certainly not too easy, also because this treatment is repugnant and disgusting. For me, it would be no small humiliation to have to seek new help.

In addition, I have an ulcer that I treat very well with the thermal water that I find in this area, and works very well on me.

Finally, I also froze my feet and because of the good local climate, especially in winter, I do not suffer much.

In view of these evils that plague me for which I can provide a documentation to prove it, I would like to allow myself to disagree with my transfer to Manoppello and ask to stay in Caramanico.

I think this is the first time in my life that I allow myself to make this request to one of my superiors.

That's why I ask you to do this charity for me, considering I'm old.

In the hope that I will not be denied this charity, I kiss your hand and ask for your blessing.

P. Domenico da Cese

The mayor, just like the doctor and the father guardian, lined up in his favor speaking to the Provincial; even the citizens of Caramanico gathered signatures for a petition addressed to the Provincial asking to let him stay there. In vain!

Padre Domenico obeyed and left the town.

From the residence certificate we know that Padre Domenico left Caramanico on the 13th of July, 1967 and that, four days later, on July 17th, he was already a resident in Manoppello; actually, as we can see later, he was already in Manoppello before that day.

If the beginning of his stay in Caramanico seemed like a mild sunrise, so the end became a sunset.

On the left: Padre Domenico in prayer.

For those who love God,

every thing

must serve

to its best.

Padre Domenico's prayers were not answered. He was not allowed to hear confessions at first, nor to stay in Caramanico Terme. He obeyed and went where he was ordered, in Manoppello.

No one could have imagined that, already in the previous years, God had purified, worked, polished Padre Domenico from Cese like a precious stone, to use now as his tool.

He only knew that:

> *"In the cross there is salvation.*
>
> *In the cross there is victory!*
>
> *be greeted cross, only hope!"*

On March 22, 1967 Father Giovanni Rosso called from Assisi to Manoppello to ask the father guardian if Padre Domenico could accompany a group of pilgrims of the "Pro Civitate Christiana" to the Holy Land as a confessor. The father forwarded the request to the Provincial, who sent an urgent request to Rome to the General Father. On March 24th all the authorizations were already approved.

The same day, March 22, 1967, Padre Domenico received from the Bishop Giovanni Battista Bosio the authorization (and the related document) to administer the confession in Manoppello and in Lettomanoppello.

A great gift!

After six months he was again allowed to help souls to reconcile with God through confession!

No one thought that shortly after in Israel would have broken out the Six-Day War. But for Padre Domenico, Israel's situation was secondary at this moment.

He must have lived a moment of unforgettable loveliness in Bethlehem, celebrating the Holy Mass where Jesus Christ was born, where the Word was made flesh, right there!

After what happened he could join the choir of angels singing, "Glory to God in the highest heavens!"

Once again, he could experience personally that "Christ, our Savior, is with us!"

He proclaimed the glory of God, and now he felt even more a son of the celestial Father.

Even in the Holy Land he never got tired to show that love comes from the top, from the Father.

In the pictures, he looks like he wants to hold out his hand to God so that He can fill it with His blessing. Only then could he become a dispenser of graces.

What could he have thought praying the rosary in the Garden of Gethsemane?

Maybe the image he had in front of his eyes every day in Penne, in the refectory, during novitiate reminded him: the soul must be pierced, perforated from side to side.

At the same time, he must agree to answer the purest love for the father: "Not as I want, but as you want ... Your will be done!"

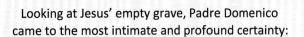

Looking at Jesus' empty grave, Padre Domenico came to the most intimate and profound certainty:

EVERYTHING leads to Jesus Christ's victory!

Hallelujah!

A short time after Padre Domenico arrived at the convent in Manoppello, the inhabitants of the town already started talking to each other, whispering: *"We have received a saint!"* This is what the people of Manoppello told me. He became a "father" for many of them. Once again, the followers came from far away to ask for his advice about all kinds of things or to confess. Often grandparents would bring to him their grandchildren and relatives to have them blessed by him.

Pictures from the year 1966 show him celebrating a mass for a golden wedding anniversary – 50 years of the sacrament of marriage!

It didn't matter if it concerned marriages, first communions, confession, or to bless a car or a meeting… he was always there, for everyone. Below, on the right he blesses a car with Padre Gaudenzio who was the first one taking him to Manoppello.

Who would have imagined that just a little earlier he wrote to the Provincial about his "old age" and his several illnesses? He was needed, and he was there.

Padre Domenico was a real blessing for many, for instance: deaf-mute people, sick, families, couples and children.

Giuseppe Orlando told me about his first experiences with Padre Domenico. Anna Maria, his fiancé, one day told him she wanted to introduce him to the Padre. He agreed.

So, they went together to Manoppello and both talked for almost an hour with Padre Domenico. At the end of the meeting the Padre suggested Giuseppe to say a mass for his grandmother Maria Grazia. He asked astonished: ***"But who is she? I don't have any grandmother with that name."*** Padre Domenico told him not to ask questions but to just say a mass for her. Giuseppe had someone celebrate a holy mass for Maria Grazia. He thought maybe the Padre was mistaken and that he meant someone else.

But he wanted to get to the bottom of the situation. Once home he researched and he learned from his mother that his paternal grandmother died when his father was just 5 years old. Her name was Maria Grazia. At home they never talked about it because his father did not remember her anymore.

Another time Giuseppe went to the sanctuary to confess. He stayed almost half an hour in the confessional.

The weird thing, though, was that Padre Domenico was the only one talking. He listed a series of things he had to confess and leave behind; then he also listed the virtues in which he had to practice on with determination so that he could grow in the love of God.

At the end of the confession, Giuseppe could say that for the first time in his life he was able to really get to know himself:

"I was a man full of flaws and bad habits, I loved everything I liked and that was usually sinful...But Padre Domenico made me a spiritual man."

"We were so happy when, on December 8, 1975, he celebrated our wedding mass, in Manoppello.

Every time he met us, the Padre exclaimed:

"Here they are, my favorite children!"

For Padre Domenico everything pointed towards the only real essential
element: the "Holy Eucharist."
All his life was shaped by it; it was the heartbeat of his existence.

The President of "Italian National Union for the transport of Sick people to Lourdes and International Sanctuaries" (UNITALSI) asked the Provincial if Padre Domenico could accompany the ill people on a pilgrimage by train to Lourdes from September 25 to October 2, 1967. The Provincial forwarded the request to the General Father, who was in Rome, with a letter dated September 2, 1967. The General consented with a letter dated September 6, 1967 (see the documents below).

UNIONE NAZIONALE ITALIANA TRASPORTO AMMALATI A LOURDES E SANTUARI D'ITALIA

- ROMA -

SEZIONE ROMANA

ROMA, ...
Via della Pigna, 13/a - Telef. 684.939

Prot. n. ....
Allegati n. ....

Rev.do Padre Guardiano
dei Cappuccini del Santuario
del Volto Sahto

Manoppello

Si dichiara che il Rev.do Padre Domenico Petracca prenderà parte come Assistente Spirituale al prossimo pellegrinaggio a Lourdes da noi organizzato dal 25 Settembre al 2 Ottobre p.v. Distinti saluti

Il Presidente

FR. CLEMENTINO DA VLISSINGEN
DI TUTTO L'ORDINE DEI FF. MINORI CAPPUCCINI DI S. FRANCESCO
MINISTRO GENERALE (n. i.)

Al diletto figlio nel Signore R.P.Domenico da Cese
della Provincia di Abruzzo

SALUTE NEL SIGNORE

In virtù della presente e col merito della santa obbedienza, Le permettiamo di recarsi a LOURDES, per sacro ministero.

A tale effetto Le accordiamo un discreto e conveniente spazio di tempo, trascorso il quale, sarà sollecita di fare ritorno al Convento di sua dimora.
Inoltre con la presente La raccomandiamo a coloro, presso i quali Le occorrerà di recarsi, affinché da essi sia benevolmente accolta e ammessa alla celebrazione della Santa Messa.
L'Angelo del Signore La accompagni nel suo viaggio ed Ella preghi per Noi che di tutto cuore la benediciamo.

Roma, dalla Nostra Curia Generalizia   6 settembre 1967

Ministro Generale OFMCap.

In Lourdes he could lead people to the very special grace of his life, to Mary. Countless times he had experienced her help.

During the pilgrimage he could make new friends and deepen the friendship with people who then accompanied him until his death: Agostina Lazzarini and Mr. Sante Burchi.

In 1968, it was requested again if Padre Domenico could accompany pilgrims to Lourdes. But in the documents a permission released by the General Father could not be found. One year later though, on September 12, 1969, our Padre Domenico went to Lourdes once again.

Pray, bathe and confess.

They are the remedies that the Holy Virgin Mary herself, the Mother of Our Lord, revealed to Bernadette Soubirous appearing in the grotto as the Immaculate Conception. Through this the soul and the body can find the original purity again, the grace of baptism! In the picture below right, Padre Domenico with Mr. Sante Burchi.

Pictures of the pilgrimage to Lourdes in 1969.

Picture of the pilgrimage to Lourdes in 1972

"Man hu? - What is it?" The Israelites once asked themselves when, after 40 years of wandering in the desert, they found around their tents "angels' food" able to satisfy their hunger (Ex 16:15). With a little imagination we can imagine that Padre Domenico had similar feelings when contemplating the Holy Face in the Church of the Capuchins' Convent (which since 2006 has been named "Basilica del Volto Santo"). Every day, he spent many hours in front of the veil, face to face with Jesus Christ.

In the Holy Face, the image of the face of Our Lord is visible and at the same time transparent – according to the light source – and is imprinted on an extremely thin cloth – Man hu? What is that? A spider web?! This image is so delicate, so fine and subtle, that it can only be compared to a spider's web.

This was for Padre Domenico an enlightenment: he continued to talk about spider webs, he could not know about sea-silk. Only later, in 2005, Dorothea Link, was the first to identify the material and recognized it: sea byssus!

In his adoring contemplation of the Volto Santo (Holy Face), Padre Domenico realized that this was not the face of a dead man; in fact, it shows a certain vivacity, not otherwise explicable or attributable to the difference between the front and the rear.

Everything you see depends on the light and the perspective of the viewer: Jesus said, *"I am the light of the world"* (Jn 8,12).

But when is the image of Jesus on this cloth dating? It must have had something to do with the Passion of Jesus because there are wounds. Is it perhaps the shroud of Veronica?

And so, Padre Domenico began his research on the Holy Face.

The altar of Veronica in Manoppello (photo on the left) shows Veronica's encounter with Jesus on the road to Calvary. How did she meet him?

Perhaps Jesus already wore the crown of thorns on his head as he dragged the cross on the road to Calvary? In this case, the thorns would have closed the wounds. If he did not wear the crown of thorns, his forehead would be torn and his wounds open and bleeding.

If Jesus had worn the crown of thorns at the time of the meeting with Veronica, there would have been holes in the cloth. But it is not so. If he had not worn it, traces of blood and open wounds would be visible on the cloth.

But the Holy Face is absolutely transparent, so it is not stained with blood and sticky. Not even on the forehead are open wounds due to the crown of thorns. This proves that the Holy Face is not the veil of Veronica.

Man hu – But then what is that?

Padre Domenico continued his research. There is still another image of the face of Jesus: The Shroud of Turin, which Secondo Pia photographed for the first time in 1898.

By the end of the 19th Century this photo was a blow to movements such as Freemasonry, Socialism and Communism, whose proponents believed that Jesus was only an invention of the Church useful to "appease" the people, to use the words of Hermann Hesse. With his photo, Secondo Pia provided proof that Jesus really existed, that he suffered and died. The Shroud was the proof.

If the two faces of Turin and Manoppello, coincided, thought Padre Domenico, one could prove that the image we see in the Holy Face is truly of Jesus.

In both faces you can see: a high forehead, one side of the face bulging and another thinner, a dark spot (hematoma) on the right side of the nose that is long and thin. Today we know that both veils had been laid on the same face.

But there are also differences: in the Turin Shroud the wound on the right, above the eye, is open and filled with blood (in white on the photo). In the Holy Face, however, there is a new grown skin. The wound is closed. In Turin the wounds of the thorns on the forehead are open, in the Holy Face they are only slightly to be seen.

In the Turin Shroud the mouth appears a little less open than it appears in the Holy Face.

MAN HU?

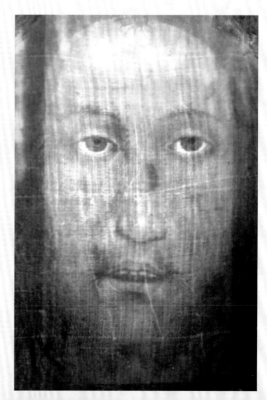

We like to think that it was at Easter, reading John's Gospel, that Padre Domenico da Cese sensed, always by the grace of God, what the Holy Face is.

John's Gospel 20,1-10:

"Now on the first day of the week Mary Magdalene came to the tomb early, while it was still dark, and saw that the stone had been taken away from the tomb. So she ran and went to Simon Peter and the other disciple, the one whom Jesus loved, and said to them, "They have taken the Lord out of the tomb, and we do not know where they have laid him." So Peter went out with the other disciple, and they were going toward the tomb. Both of them were running together, but the other disciple outran Peter and reached the tomb first. And stooping to look in, he saw the linen cloths lying there, but he did not go in. Then Simon Peter came, following him, and went into the tomb. He saw the linen cloths lying there, and the face cloth, which had been on Jesus' head, not lying with the linen cloths but folded up in a place by itself. Then the other disciple, who had reached the tomb first, also went in, and he saw and believed; for as yet they did not understand the Scripture, that he must rise from the dead. Then the disciples went back to their homes."

"This is it!" Padre Domenico guessed that the sudarium placed on Jesus' face in the tomb is in fact the Holy Face and it shows the first moment of the Resurrection.

John was the only one of the disciples to stay under the cross together with Mary. Only he saw what Jesus was like when he died. He knew all the wounds: the slightly open mouth, the hematoma on the nose, the blood from the crown of thorns ...

John saw His face not as we see him in the Shroud, he really had seen his dead Lord's face.

So God prepared him. Only he was able to "read," in the sudarium, the changes that occurred in the face of Jesus. Through this he knew that Christ was resurrected; therefore, only John could write about himself "He saw and believed."

Peter was also in the grave. He saw exactly the same as John. But he could not understand the "First Gospel of the Resurrection" because he had not stayed under the cross.

But why did John not write that he had seen the face of the resurrected Jesus in that cloth?

In the Jewish world a person who had lost a lot of blood was considered unclean; so, every person who died on the cross was cursed. Moreover, the corpse and the tomb itself were also impure. In the Sacred Scriptures the most impure quote is the one in which the Resurrection takes place.

No one would have believed him if he had written that in a tomb there was a face cloth which is the proof of the resurrection of Jesus Christ. Therefore, John wrote: "for as yet they did not understand the Scripture, that he must rise from the dead." With this he explains: I recognized the resurrection and I believed on the basis not of Scripture but of the sudarium.

The Holy Face made Padre Domenico understand, even more profoundly, the great mystery of the Eucharist.

Pius XII wrote that the celebration of the Holy Mass is the memorial of the redemption of Jesus. Thus, the presbytery (the altar) represents the tomb. Therefore, originally the altar cloths were always more than four meters long, the same length as the Shroud of Turin. In the moment of transubstantiation, Jesus returns to life and resurrection takes place. The corporal, the 'four times folded cloth' – as the Holy Face was called in ancient times – shows the transition from death to life.

For this reason, the faithful people pray here: We proclaim your death, O Lord, and profess your resurrection until you come again.

Altare Maggiore

The holy communion, then, is the encounter with the Risen Lord, in which Jesus enters personally into the soul of each faithful. — It happens now as then, in the first Easter, each one recognizes Jesus in a different way: Mary recognized him when he said her name, Thomas looking at the wounds, the disciples of Emmaus at the breaking of the bread ...

Jesus has become not the cloth but the "bread of life" for each of us. Thus, He can shape each soul individually. In fact, the soul is more delicate than a spider's web. It is absolutely true what the Curé of Ars, Saint John Vianney, said: "He looks at me and I look at him," this is true adoration!

The Holy Face becomes a key to unlock the understanding of the meaning of the celebration of Holy Mass and adoration, to deepen the reality of Jesus in the Eucharistic form.

Neither the cross nor the death of Jesus were the driving force for evangelization, because many people died like that.

The push was a completely different, inconceivable thing, the Resurrection of Jesus: faith in the victor who trampled and destroyed sin, death, hell and the devil became the kerygma.

Who builds on the rock of the victory of Jesus Christ, can stand against all the storms of life. He also wins when he loses - like the martyrs.

This is why Padre Domenico could give men the greatest comfort: the great message of the Holy Face.

So, Padre Domenico led all the faithful to the Holy Face. He never tired of directing the souls to the Risen One.

From then on, he was always and only seen with the Holy Face in his hands.

Padre Domenico always had a very close relationship with Padre Pio da Pietrelcina (1887-1968), the Capuchin friar known and honored far beyond the borders of Italy. Padre Domenico had already met him in 1940, on a visit to San Giovanni Rotondo (page 30).

Padre Pio, who possessed among other things the gift of reading souls and carried the stigmata from 1918, immediately recognized in him a spiritual son.

If Padre Domenico went to Padre Pio's other times (as well as in 1940), we do not know (Agostina Lazzarini spoke about it). Padre Pio, however, always knew in which convent Padre Domenico was, as witnessed by Fra Vincenzo da Pescara (photo on the left).

Padre Pio always sent the faithful to his spiritual son, giving them precise directions on where to go (as told on page 49).

This also happened to Clarice Marchionni (pictured right) who went to Padre Pio and was told: *"Why do you not go to Padre Domenico in the Abruzzi and save the whole trip? He is just like me!"* New on her testimony is the addition that Padre Pio said: *"He is just like me!".*

93

On September 20, 1968, it was the 50th anniversary of the stigmata, Padre Pio celebrated Mass. Two days later, on September 22, 1968 he celebrated again with his numerous prayer groups. At the end he collapsed to the ground, exhausted.

Nevertheless, he spent all day at the confessional. On the September 23, 1968 at 2:30 a.m. he died. Three days later, on September 26th, thousands of people from all over the world accompanied him on his last journey.

Both events, the collapse in the morning of Padre Pio's last day and his funeral, were closely connected with Padre Domenico.

Padre Domenico himself recounted what happened on September 22, 1968. *"Early in the morning, after opening the church [before 6 a.m., note from the writer], I was going to my place in the choir to pray.*

But Padre Pio was sitting in my place. Amazed, I asked him: "Padre Pio, what are you doing here?" And he replied: "I do not have faith in myself any longer, pray for me." And they prayed together. Then Padre Pio said: *"We will meet again in Paradise!"* And Padre Domenico: "May Jesus Christ be praised!" but Padre Pio had disappeared.

It was exactly the hour when Padre Pio was celebrating in San Giovanni Rotondo — about 200 km away — for his spiritual children of the prayer groups. How could he be in Manoppello?

From 1905, Padre Pio possessed the gift of bilocation, which means that he could be in two places at the same time; of this we have countless testimonies.

That morning was his last bilocation (see Tirelli, Roberto: Maria meets Padre Pio in Udine in Bilocation, 2006, page 36).

I have often wondered why a Father on the path to sainthood would say: *"I do not have faith in myself any longer?"*

Father Leonardo (right, bottom) — who was a deacon at the time of the last Mass of Padre Pio — confirmed to me that he had fallen to the ground, on the altar, just before 6 o'clock.

At that moment Padre Pio began the journey through the "Valley of Death." It is not our merits that open the gates of heaven but only Jesus Christ. *"No one comes to the Father except through me"* (Jn 14: 6).

Padre Pio came to Manoppello with the purpose to look at the face of Jesus the Victor who would wait for him at the threshold of eternity in the early morning.

But that is not all. When, a couple of years ago, the RAI (The Italian national TV) made the footage "The funeral of Padre Pio" available on the internet, many did not believe their eyes. That's Padre Domenico there!? (Photo below).

When Father Enrico Carusi, the guardian at that time, asked Padre Domenico to attend Padre Pio's funeral in San Giovanni Rotondo on September 26th, he replied no, because that day at Manoppello he had to lead groups of pilgrims (bottom right, his sworn testimony). A couple of days after the funeral, a group of pilgrims arrived at Manoppello. A woman asked Padre Domenico: ***"Why did you not respond, when I saw you and greeted you in San Giovanni Rotondo?"*** Padre Domenico remained silent. But as she insisted, the Father deviated the conversation by saying, ***"Now I have to accompany the pilgrims"*** and left.

The woman thought she was wrong. But both the TV footage and the sworn testimony of Father Enrico show that she was right. Even the bus driver who had brought pilgrims from Manoppello to San Giovanni Rotondo for Padre Pio's funeral declared that Padre Domenico had not left with them and was not on the bus. The following can be deduced:

Padre Domenico had the gift of bilocation as Padre Pio.

Padre Domenico is the first person who was filmed during a bilocation.

To the left: Padre Domenico during the funeral (in the oval).
Top: Sworn Statement by Father Enrico Carusi.

protected by the shadow of Padre Domenico, a new lily of great purity and beauty blossomed for e Church: Sister Amalia di Rella. She was born in Ruvo di Puglia (Bari) on May 25, 1934; as a child she anted to become a nun, but her parents and her brothers prevented her from doing so. Jesus made her nderstand that she had to consecrate herself to God by living in the world and not behind the walls of a nvent.

Since then she began a Calvary of diseases and hospitalizations. In the deepest part of her soul she felt the call: "Be a servant of the Cross by serving those who carry the Cross."

The corridors of the hospital became her convent: she stood beside the elderly, the disabled, the sick …

She found an apartment near the Church of Purgatory of Ruvo di Puglia where for over thirty years she had found refuge – at the foot of a great portrait of her beloved: the image of the Holy Face of Jesus. Here she often gathered in prayer.

In 1970, on a pilgrimage to the Holy Face of Manoppello, she met Padre Domenico da Cese for the first time.

This meeting changed her life. Padre Domenico became for her "The channel of the divine light": she had found her spiritual father, the master able to reveal the meaning of her suffering. The signs of Christ's martyrdom were imprinted on the body of the Capuchin.

Sister Amalia experienced years of intense spiritual communion with her "Father and spiritual Master." The culminating point occurred in 1972 with the following event:

The visit of Padre Domenico to Ruvo di Puglia during which the Association of the Holy Face was founded.

The Father entrusted the direction of this community to Sister Amalia.

In 1972, the bishop entrusted the task of extraordinary spiritual director of this community to Padre Domenico.

When they talked on the phone, they sometimes sang to each other: "Evviva Maria - Maria Evviva!"

They were united in Christ as father and daughter.

The following years were an alternation of joy and thanksgiving:

On February 11, 1976, the day of the Feast of Our Lady of Lourdes, Sister Amalia and Sister Maria Matera pledged in front of the Holy Face of Manoppello to dedicate themselves to God, according to the example of St. Francis. What they desired in the years of their youth, but had been denied for so long, was finally fulfilled!

As his spiritual daughter, she would be at Padre Domenico's bedside in Turin while he was dying, and to the wake and funeral, in Manoppello.

In 1979, the Crucifix appeared to Sister Amalia and she received a wound on her left hand.

In 1981, the year of her religious profession, she also received the stigma on her right hand.

On May 13, 1985, the secular institute founded by her "The Pious Disciples of the Holy Face of Jesus" was officially recognized by the Church.

On June 16, 1994, she died in her hometown, Ruvo di Puglia, thus returning to the house of the Father.

Padre Domenico lived in friendship with Jesus, his whole life was shaped by it. This attracted people. One of them was the psychiatrist and psychologist Bruno Sammaciccia (1926-2013) who came from a completely different world. In 1956, as he himself told, he had an experience with UFOs and since then he considered himself a "ufologist". We do not know how and why he went to Padre Domenico. It must have been him who had brought him to the Holy Face. Sammaciccia was fascinated by the image of Christ and also by Padre Domenico.

And so, the scientist discovered a new dimension, the religious one.

Thanks to him the first scientific inquiries on the Holy Face began.

The longer Sammaciccia spent time with Padre Domenico, the more his affection for him grew.

To him we owe many photos of Padre Domenico from the 1970s.

Bruno Sammaciccia organized conferences and lectures on the Holy Face in which Padre Domenico always took part.

June 6, 1973

Conference held June 20, 1974 in the Hotel "Casa del Pellegrino", Manoppello.

In the group of researchers there was also a Passionist, Fr. Enrico Sammarco (pictured above) who, in 1972, wrote a book entitled "Recalling the Holy Face of Manoppello," in which the first results of the research were published.

In 1974, Sammaciccia and Padre Domenico carried out a Wood's lamp examination on the Holy Face. This lamp emits an ultraviolet light with which the presence of color can be detected. The examination showed that there is no trace of color on the Holy Face. This was reported by Bruno Sammaciccia in his book, "The Holy Face of Jesus in Manoppello: hypothesis, research, reflections, documentations, Assisi, 1974."

Sammaciccia also commissioned Prof. Giorgio Baitello (1908-1995) to investigate the Holy Face. The scholar of art came to the conclusion that *"that face and veil constituted a true miracle."* In the picture below on the right, Padre Domenico shows him the Holy Face.

In 1977, S.E. Stanislao Battistelli, Bishop Emeritus of Teramo and Atri, Passionist, and Prof. Giorgio Baitello, visited the Holy Face and had the veil explained by Padre Domenico.

The Bishop Battistelli (1885-1981), who was then more than 90 years old, was a worshiper of the Holy Face. From 1932 to 1952 he was the Bishop of Savana-Pitigliano, and from 1952 to 1967 he was leading the diocese of Teramo-Atri.

Prof. Baitello, an art scholar, had already examined the Holy Face a few years earlier, at the request of Sammaciccia.

At this inspection were present:

Prof. Giorgio Baitello, Fr. Pietro, Bruno Sammaciccia, Fr. Luciano; Mons. Stanislao Battistelli, Fr. Clemente and Padre Domenico (from the left to right).

Bruno Sammaciccia

P. DOMENICO DEL VOLTO SANTO
CAPPUCCINO

MISTICO ESPIRATO TAUMATURGO

Bruno Sammaciccia was also a writer: in 1972, he published a book on the "Eucharistic Miracle" of Lanciano.

In 1974, a volume of historical-scientific character was published on the Holy Face followed by a second edition, totally revised and corrected, in 1978.

He also published a short note on the scientific results on the Holy Face.

In 1979, he also published a biography of Padre Domenico, which was amended and reprinted in 1990 (left).

On the occasion of the 19th National Eucharistic Congress, which was held in Pescara from September 11 to 18, 1977, Padre Domenico organized an exhibition on the Holy Face with the help of Bruno Sammaciccia. Pope Paul VI in person attended the congress in Pescara.

Padre Domenico was of the opinion that only the one who understood that he could meet Jesus, the Risen One, through the Eucharistic guise can truly celebrate the Holy Mass. For this he wanted to draw attention to the Holy Face. In this congress, Renzo Allegri met for the first time the Holy Face on which he drew the attention of the press.

The more they cooperated together, the more Bruno Sammaciccia's affection for Padre Domenico grew. He invited him to his house, in Assisi, to celebrate his birthday.

Jesus recognizes the emotions of the hearts of people. Padre Domenico also had the gift of reading souls. He welcomed every single person God sent to him and took them into his prayers. How great his intercession was will only be known in eternity.

Everyone, however, is responsible for how he manages his freedom.

Two of Padre Domenico's closest collaborators were his niece Caterina Petracca (right) and Agostina Lazzarini (left). Caterina is the daughter of his brother Angelo and she was married to the photographer Franco Di Lorenzo, who is also the author of this photo.

Caterina Petracca (pictured below with her husband Franco) lived in trust of God. In 1981, her faith was severely tested when her husband, Franco Di Lorenzo, became ill with pancreatic cancer. After two surgeries and three months hospitalization, he had dropped from 187 pounds to only 66 pounds. When a third surgery was scheduled, Franco had heard the doctor say, "Why do you bring me a man who is about to die?"

Because Caterina Petracca, his wife, did not know what to do anymore, she put a picture of Padre Domenico under his pajamas. Franco took it and prayed: *"Padre Domenico, help me, otherwise I will die!"*

Then one day Franco saw in a vision the bust of Padre Domenico, who did not say anything. Then he saw Pope John XXIII talking to him: *"Through the intercession of Padre Domenico you will heal."* From that moment on, he no longer felt any pain and did not need medication anymore. He was healed!

At Christmas he could even toast with sparkling wine. In the documentary by Paul Badde on the life of Padre Domenico ("Baddes Bilder") Franco says: *"I live and I wanted to live."*

Franco, a professional photographer, collected and processed the photos of Padre Domenico – which were used for this volume. He died in the spring of 2018 and said that Padre Domenico was the "Padre Pio of the Abruzzi."

Agostina Lazzarini (pictured here on the right) was born in Bologna on June 18, 1921. In 1946, she became a spiritual daughter of Padre Pio who, in 1959, addressed her to Padre Domenico.

She was not married and had entered the Franciscan tertiary with the name of Sister Agostina. She lived in Teramo, together with another tertiary; and every Sunday she went to see Padre Domenico. He took care of her soul while she provided for his material needs.

She reported being cured from an ulcer in 1960; ten years later, in 1970, her father was healed from kidney cancer.

Agostina remained close to Padre Domenico until his death, helping him in everything she could.

It was she who wrote the first biography of Padre Domenico and Bruno Sammaciccia took her manuscript as the basis for his book on him.

In her book, Agostina relates an interesting thing: Padre Domenico often went to see Padre Pio; we do not know, however, whether personally or in bilocation.

When, in 1984, Pope John Paul II visited Teramo, Sister Agostina gave him 76 boxes with documents about Padre Pio and Padre Domenico, Sammaciccia's book on the life of Padre Domenico and several photos.

Later she wrote many letters to the Pope (an example in the photo on the right) in which she attached testimonies on Padre Domenico. Unfortunately, there was no trace of this correspondence in the Vatican.

We can therefore assume Pope John Paul II, when he received the letters of Agostina, already knew the life of Padre Domenico.

As the Holy Face became more and more known, the need arose to have informative material and holy cards with prayers available to the faithful who wanted to know more.

SEGRETERIA DI STATO

N. 154791/A   DAL VATICANO, 13 Luglio 1985

Gentile Sig.a,

In occasione della recente visita pastorale del Sommo Pontefice alla città di Teramo, Ella ha voluto rivolgerGli un indirizzo di devoto omaggio, accompagnandolo con alcuni scritti di argomento religioso e con un'offerta (Lire 200.000), destinata in pari entità ad un bambino polacco ed a un suo coetaneo africano.

Il Santo Padre, come ha gradito i devoti sentimenti da Lei manifestati, così ha apprezzato la sua generosa intenzione a favore di due piccoli fratelli più bisognosi di aiuto.

Nel manifestarLe, a mio mezzo, riconoscenza per l'attestato di venerazione e di carità operante, Sua Santità invoca l'effusione dei favori celesti, in pegno dei quali invia la propiziatrice Sua Benedizione.

Con sensi di distinta stima

dev.mo nel Signore

(Mons.G.B.Re, Assessore)

Gent.ma Sig.a
AGOSTINA LAZZARINI

TERAMO

Padre Domenico began, with the help of Caterina and Agostina, to write notes and prepare leaflets and have them translated in various languages:

Italian, English, French and German.

there, and the handkerchief which had been about his head, not lying with the linen cloths, but folded in a place by itself. Then the other disciple also went in, who had come first to the tomb. And he saw and believed; for as yet they did not understand the Scripture, that he must rise from the dead. The disciples therefore went away again to their home. Nobody can deny the existence of the sudarium that vovered the Face of Jesus after His death.

YOUR BLOOD SOAKED EVERYTHING O LORD. AND THUS MYSTICALLY AND PRODIGIOUSLY YOUR HOLY FACE REMAINED IMPRESSED ON THE VEIL OF MANOPPELLO.

Who really has faith in Jesus, feels and sees in this Holy Face the living presence of the Divine Redeemer.

BLESSING OF JESUS

Our Lord Jesus
look at me and bless me
and turn your face
towards me
O Lord Jesus
have mercy on me
and give me peace
O Lord Jesus
give me your holy blessing
and deliver me from evil.

P. DOMENICO CAPPUCCINO
Santuario del Volto Santo - tel. 857.11.18
65024 Manoppello (PE)

Il Volto Santo di MANOPPELLO

Holy Face of Jesus
of MANOPPELLO

A PRAYER TO THE HOLY FACE

Oh, Jesus, who in bitter suffering were hated by men and became a man of sorrows, I venerate your divine face, on wich the grace and sweetness of divinity used to shine, and wich has now become for me like the face of a leper.

But underneath these deformed looks, I perceive your infinite love, and am consumed by the desire to love you and to make all men love you.

The tears which well up from your eyes are to me like gracious pearls which I love to gather, so that with their infinite value I can buy back the souls of sinners.

Oh, Jesus, whose face is the only beauty which enraptures my heart, I accept that I cannoy see the sweetness of your eyes here on Earth, nor feel the ineffable kiss of your lips; but oh! I beg you to imprint in me your divine likeness, to fire me with your love so that I am quinckly consumed by it and so come soon to see your glorious face in Heaven. Amen.

Indulgence of 500 days applicable also to souls in Purgatory.

PIUS X - 13th Feb. 1906

Veil brought by Angelic hands to Manoppello in 1506

HOLY FACE OF JESUS

In the year 1506, an Angel of God delivered to Dr. Giacomantonio Leonelli, the mysterious image of the Holy Face of Jesus and said: «Keep this devotion very dear and God will give you many favors, and will give you prosperity, both temporal and spiritual». After those words, the Angel of God, under the appearance of a pilgrim disappeared and everything remained a most dense mystery.

WHAT IS THE HOLY FACE OF MANOPPELLO?

According to the opinions and the statements of the faithful that are by the thousands in the world, and according to experts and men of great intellect, according also to great ecclesiastics, and many religious, this Holy Face is precisely that linen sudarium, was the one of Magdalene, the first woman that went to the sepulchre and said: «I saw the Tomb of the living Christ risen, the glory of Christ risen, the Angels, his testimony and the sudarium that was placed on the Face of Jesus».

The Gospel according to St. John: Peter therefore went out, and the other disciple, and they went to the tomb. The two were running together, and the other disciple ran on before, faster than Peter, and came first to the tomb. And stooping down he saw the linen cloths lying there, yet he did not enter. Simon Peter therefore came following him, and he went into the tomb, and saw the linen cloths lying

When translations were needed Mrs. Veronika Zach helped with the German language (photo).

She was originally from Switzerland as her husband Martin; both rented an apartment in a house owned by Bruno Sammaciccia.

Mrs. Zach became a spokesperson for Padre Domenico in the German speaking countries.

Below we see some of her translations.

Ich will dass Du jede Stunde des Tages und der Nacht an mich denkst; ich will dass Du auch die geringste Tat nur aus Liebe machst. Ich zähle auf Dich, um mich zu freuen.

Es soll Dich nicht betrüben, wenn Du keine Tugenden hast, ich werde Dir die meinigen geben.

Wenn Du leiden solltest, werde ich Dir die Kraft geben. Mir hast Du die Liebe gegeben; ich werde Dich lieben lernen, mehr als Du erträumst.

Aber erinnere Dich..... Liebe mich, wie Du bist.

Ich habe Dir meine Mutter gegeben; lass alles durch ihr reines Herz gehen. Was immer auch geschehen möge, warte nicht ab, ein Heiliger zu werden, um Dich der Liebe hinzugeben, so würdest Du mich nie lieben.

(M. Lebrun von E.M.T.)

Gebet zum heiligen Antlitz

Oh Jesus Christus, der Du in Deiner bitteren Passion zur Schmach der Menschheit und zum Schmerzensreichen geworden bist, ich verehre Dein göttliches Antlitz, das die Sanftheit der Göttlichkeit wiederspiegelt, und das heute für mich wie das eines Aussätzigen geworden ist!

Aber unter diesem entstellten Aussehen, entdecke ich eine unendliche Liebe und ich verzehre mich im Wunsch, Dich zu lieben und Dich von jedem Menschen lieben zu lassen.

Die Tränen, die aus Deinen Augen fliessen, scheinen mir wie kostbare Perlen, die ich sammeln möchte, um mit ihrem unschätzbaren Wert, die Seelen der Sünder loszukaufen.

Oh Jesus Christus, dessen Angesicht die einzige Schönheit ist die mein Herz bezaubert, ich will in diesem Leben gerne auf mich nehmen, die Sanftheit Deines Blickes nicht zu sehen, den unermesslichen Kuss Deines Mundes nicht zu fühlen; aber ich flehe Dich an, in mir Deine göttliche Ähnlichkeit einzuprägen, mich an Deiner Liebe zu entzünden, damit diese mich in kurzer Zeit verzehre und es mir recht

---

bald vergönnt ist, Dein glorreiches Antlitz im Himmel zu sehen.

Amen.

Ablass von 500 Tagen, auch für die Seelen des Fegefeuers anwendbar.

Pius X   13. Februar 1906

Der Schleier wurde im Jahre 1506 von Engelshand nach Manoppello gebracht.

Psalm 67

Rit.

Erhebe Dein Angesicht auf uns, oh Herr,
    der Herr sei uns gnädig und segne uns,
Lass leuchten sein Angesicht über uns
auf dass der Erde Dein Weg und Dein Heil bekannt werde unter allen Menschen. (Rit.)
Es loben Dich die Völker, oh Gott, es loben Dich die Völker alle. Es freuen sich und es jubeln die Menschen, weil Du die Welt mit Gerechtigkeit regierst. Richte gerecht die Nationen und die Völker der Erde führe zum Heil! (Rit.)
Es loben Dich die Völker, oh Gott, es loben Dich die Völker alle; die Erde hat ihre Früchte gegeben.
Segne uns oh Gott, unser Gott, und es fürchten ihn alle Regionen der Erde. (Rit.)

SEGEN

Der Herr Jesus segne und behüte mich,
und erhebe sein Angesicht auf mich,
der Herr Jesus habe Erbarmen mit mir.
und gebe mir den Frieden;
der Herr Jesus gebe mir seinen heiligen Segen
und erlöse mich von allem Bösen....
    Amen.

Hochwürden PATER DOMENICO
Heiligtum des heiligen Antlitzes - Tel. 8.57.11.18
85024 MANOPPELLO (PE) ITALIEN
mit kirchlicher Genehmigung

Es ist ein hauchdünnes Linnen, fast ein Schleier lischer Erscheinung, der die Gesichtszüge des Erlösers in lebendigem Ausdruck trägt, dessen töne im Laufe der Jahrhunderte nichts von ihr eingebüsst haben und von Menschenhand wurden. Durch einen Engel wurde das Tüchlein n ppello gebracht im Jahre 1506.

ICH BIN DEIN GOTT.

N DEIN GOTT,
ich bin Dir nahe, genügt es Dir nicht? Was willst auf der Erde mehr, als das was mein Herz erfüllt?

N DEIN GOTT,
bleibe Dir treu, auch wenn ich Dir das Kreuz gen muss; und wie schwer es auch ist, erinnere ich bin bei Dir, was willst Du mehr?

DEIN GOTT,
denke an Dich .... aus der Ewigkeit habe ich an dacht. Ich habe Deinen Namen im Grunde meines geschrieben.

DEIN GOTT,
ordne alles zu Deinem Besten; wenn Du es heute erstehen kannst, eines Tages wirst Du es mit wissen.

DEIN GOTT,
ich liebe Dich getreu; ich kenne alles, was Dich drückt; ich sehe jeden Blick, ich höre Deines Wort, en Dich ist. Nimm alles mit Ruhe und Frieden an. es so geplant habe; fahre fort, bleibe mir treu, ein Herz Dich belohne.

DEIN GOTT,
Du allein, ich bin bei Dir. Niemand hat ein gutes Dich? Komm zu mir, ich werde Dir alles im heiligen t geben; ich werde Dich entschädigen, für das auf der Erde versagt bleibt.

DEIN GOTT,
willst Du mehr? Mach Dir Mut! Es wird Dir nichts denn wer mein göttliches Herz besitzt, hat alles, benötigt. Die Welt vergeht, die Zeit flieht, die verschwinden, der Tod rafft alles hin. Nur eines immer bleiben: DEIN GOTT.

OH JESUS, DU HAST RECHT!

Ich bin das LICHT, und Du siehst mich nicht.
Ich bin der WEG, und Du folgst mir nicht.
Ich bin die WAHRHEIT, und Du glaubst mir nicht.
Ich bin das LEBEN, und Du suchst mich nicht.
Ich bin der LEHRER, und Du hörst nicht auf mich.
Ich bin der MEISTER, und Du gehorchst mir nicht.
Ich bin der FREUND, und Du liebst mich nicht.
Ich bin Dein GOTT, und Du betest nicht zu mir.
Wenn Du nicht glücklich bist, gib nicht mir die Schuld.

OH JESUS, DU HAST RECHT!

Zu wenig denke ich an Dich, zu wenig liebe ich Dich, deshalb bin ich unglücklich.

Aber Dein offenes Haus ladet mich immer ein und vergibt mir meine Sünden.

In Deinem heiligen Herz, Quelle des Lichts, finde ich immer wieder:

die KRAFT, Dir zu folgen: WEG, WAHRHEIT und LEBEN;
die GNADE, Dich anzuhören: MEISTER und LEHRER;
die FREUDE, Dich zu lieben: Gott der Liebe.
FREUND allen denen, die Dir vertrauen.

LIEBE MICH WIE DU BIST !

Ich kenne Deine Not, Dein Kampf und die Qual Deiner Seele, die Schwächen und die Leiden Deines Körpers; ich weiss von Deiner Feigheit, Deinen Sünden und ich sage Dir trotzdem :

« GIB MIR DEIN HERZ, LIEBE MICH WIE DU BIST.. »

Wenn Du erwartest ein Engel zu werden, um Dich der Liebe hinzugeben, wirst Du nie lieben. Auch wenn Du feige bist in der Pflichterfüllung und in der Tugend, wenn Du oft in jene Sünden zurückfällst, die Du nicht mehr begehen möchtest, SO ERLAUBE ICH DIR NICHT, MICH NICHT ZU LIEBEN.

LIEBE MICH WIE DU BIST.

In jeder Gemütsverfassung, sei es in der Hingabe oder in der Gleichgültigkeit, in der Treue oder in der Untreue, liebe mich wie Du bist... Ich will die Liebe Deines armseligen Herzens; wenn Du erwartest, vollkommen zu werden, wirst Du mich nie lieben.

Kann ich vielleicht nicht aus jedem Sandkorn einen Edelstein machen, leuchtend vor Reinheit und Liebe? Bin ich nicht der Allmächtige? Und wenn ich vor allen Andern die armselige Liebe Deines Herzens vorziehe, bin ich nicht Herr meiner Liebe?

Mein Sohn, lass mich Dich lieben, ich will Dein Herz. Gewiss mit der Zeit will ich Dich ändern, aber im Moment liebe ich Dich, wie Du bist.... und verlange von Dir dieselbe; ich will, dass aus der Not die Liebe geboren wird. Ich liebe in Dir auch Deine Schwächen; ich liebe die Zuneigung der Armen und Bedrängten; ich will aus dem Urgrund Deiner Seele nur eines hören: « JESUS, ICH LIEBE DICH ».

Ich will einzig und allein die Melodie Deines Herzens; ich habe weder Deine Wissenschaft noch Dein Talent nötig. Nur eines ist mir wichtig, Dich mit Liebe arbeiten zu sehen. Es sind nicht Deine Tugenden, die ich wünsche; das würde nur Deine Eigenliebe nähren; sei unbesorgt! Ich hätte Dich für grosse Dinge auserlesen können, nein Du wärst der unnütze Diener; ich werde Dir sogar noch das Wenige nehmen, das Du hast... weil ich Dich nur für die Liebe erschaffen habe....

Heute stehe ich an der Pforte Deines Herzens wie ein Bettler, ich der König der Könige! Ich klopfe an und warte; beeile Dich mir zu öffnen. Zeige mir Deine Nöte; wenn Du Deine Armut wirklich kennen würdest, müsstest Du vor Schmerz sterben.

Zweifel und Mangel an Vertrauen Deinerseits, sind die grössten Wunden meines Herzens.

Padre Domenico lived in the convent of Manoppello together with his confreres. He was aware of the challenges the lady cook had to face when unexpected guests arrived and the food available was not enough for everyone.

The cook reported that in such cases, Padre Domenico went into the kitchen, prayed and threw whatever available, for example some bread, into the pot saying: *"Do not worry, now it will be enough!"* And it was just like that.

Padre Domenico did not eat meat, he said that in the flesh there was the taste of death. His favorite dish was gnocchi with tomato sauce, according to Mrs. Zach. From time to time he drank a beer because he said it was good for the kidneys. - The first time I saw him drinking beer, I smiled to myself. But later I had to agree with Padre Domenico when a lady told me that her husband was suffering from kidney stones and that a doctor had ordered him to drink beer because of its power to dissolve them.

February 13, 1975: Padre Domenico gathered in prayer (right) at the coffin of Father Gaudenzio, the Brother who had always been a true friend and brother to him.

Father Gaudenzio had also been the one who in 1963 had brought him for the first time to Manoppello, to the Holy Face.

With some of his confreres in Manoppello: behind Padre Domenico there is the Provincial of that time and the first from the right is Fr. Clemente.

For Christmas or during other holidays, Padre Domenico went back to visit his family in Cese.

Above he was photographed in the home of his brother Angelo.

Padre Domenico at the wedding of Caterina Petracca (above) and at the one of his sister (right).

What a great emotion it was for Padre Domenico to celebrate Mass in the new church of Cese! (above)

On a visit to his brother Angelo's house (the fourth from the right).

Ida Loidl

Mrs. Ida Loidl (+ October 22, 1985), Austrian, arrived for the first time in Manoppello in 1972, with a group of pilgrims, after making a stop in nearby Lanciano. In her magazine "Grüß Gott!" (No. 9-10 of 1978) she reported her experience:

"The first time we were in Lanciano was in May 1972 (....) Lanciano is a pilgrimage destination on where the eucharistic miracle is still visible today, I asked a minor conventual friar of the place if it was true that 70 km away, in the town of Manoppello, there was a Capuchin who possessed the gift of reading souls. The minor friar answered me with a strong and energetic "Yes" adding "Padre Domenico is a saint." I thought this could be possible, but was it true that this father possessed the gift of reading deep in souls? And to be sure, I asked him once again: "… but does he possess the gift of reading souls?" And he answered me with a "Yes" even stronger and more energetic and went on to say: "In him there is something similar to Padre Pio, with the difference that accessing Padre Domenico is certainly easier than it happens with Padre Pio." I immediately decided to go on to Manoppello. Since my youth I had the desire to speak once with a true man of God to know what my soul was like before God.

Throughout the journey, I repeated my pray: "My God, if you want to tell me something through Padre Domenico, that it is really what YOU want to tell me, otherwise better don't know anything!" I did not know Padre Domenico at all, I had never met him and I did not want to hear something that was only the result of his personal opinion. When we arrived at the Sanctuary of the Holy Face, which is held by the Capuchin Fathers (...) I prayed Sister Ingonda — who was part of our group and who, as an Italian teacher, speaks well the language — to act as interpreter with Padre Domenico.

(...) While all the other pilgrims were gathered in the church for community prayer, the two of us headed to the sacristy to ask for Padre Domenico, who lives in the adjoining convent.

It did not take long for the gifted Capuchin to stand before me. I only had two questions that for me were the most important:

1. If God was happy with me.
2. If the behavior I held in life was what it was supposed to be.

(...) And in the middle of his speech he told me: "What I tell you now, I do not tell you from me, I tell you from God!"

His answers came naturally and spontaneously. Although he had never seen me before and never heard of me, his answers were as if they had been cut out for me and his affirmations reached the moment I entered eternity.

I was struck in the deepest of my soul. It was just what I had always prayed for! Through Padre Domenico, God had therefore told me the truth! When Padre Domenico handed me his hand to say goodbye and gave me his blessing, the world had completely disappeared for me. I knelt before the tabernacle, because only the Lord, in the Blessed Sacrament, could be for me at this hour all what I needed. In any case, this day was one of the most intense and the most beautiful of my life."

Photo of the group of pilgrims from Salzburg who arrived in Manoppello with Ida Loidl.

Above: Padre Domenico in conversation with Sister Ingonda Höll.

All photos were taken in front of the shrine of Manoppello.

After this first encounter with Padre Domenico, Ida Loidl returned every year to Manoppello from Salzburg, with a group of pilgrims of about 100 people.

The Prelate Ferdinand Holböck (1913-2001, photo on the left) and other priests acted as supporters and did help with the language, like Sister Ingonda Holl (1920-1982), and Veronika Zach as well, acted as translators in individual interviews or confessions.

Padre Domenico started an ever-increasing correspondence with the German faithful; Veronika Zach was always there to lend a hand to translate those letters into Italian.

But who was Ida Loidl? Although she had not completed higher studies and had a temperamental character, she was inflamed by the Holy Spirit. First, she ran a bookshop in Austria with her sister, then she founded a musical and theatrical group, with which she went around the country to strengthen people's fidelity and joy of faith.

Grüß Gott!

8. Jahrgang   Heft 11/12   November/ Dezember 1985

Alle, die es hörten, verwunderten sich über die Kunde, die ihnen die Hirten brachten !

Die Hirten kehrten zurück und lobten und priesen Gott für alles, was sie gehört und gesehen hatten, so wie es ihnen gesagt worden war.

Then she organized pilgrimages to deepen the faith; and in this period, she began to write her own books with the purpose to give people positive models.

In 1978, she began to publish the magazine, "Grüß Gott" - first only for adults, then there was an edition for young people and finally also a magazine for children.

She was the first to be surprised that the magazine, in only eight years, obtained an international resonance spreading in Austria, Germany, Switzerland, Lichtenstein, France, Portugal, Italy, Hungary, Poland, Romania, Yugoslavia, Sweden, Holland, England, Belgium, Israel, Egypt, Canada, Peru, Brazil, New Guinea, Zaire, West Africa, Argentina, Tanzania, and Ghana.

In Ghana, "Grüß Gott" was translated into the national language, as she wrote in the issue May-June 1985 (on page 85).

Since almost every year Mrs. Loidl wrote of Padre Domenico, his life, his family, his miracles, etc., our Capuchin became famous all over the world.

✠ Pater Domenico von Manoppello

2 Fortsetzung

Die gute Familie Zich, bei welcher Pater Domenico – wie bereits berichtet – en Freitagen gen'18 kurz auf Besuch gekommen war, damit ihm die Oolmetscherin, Frau Verena Zich, in deutscher Sprache erhaltene Korrespondenz übersetzen und seine Antworten dazu, hatte dadurch auch Gelegenheit, manches private Gespräch mit Pater Domenico zu führen.

Wenn in der Familie Krankheitsfälle auftauchten, gab Pater Domenico immer die richtigen Ratschläge. Von Operationen riet er meistens ab. Oft sagte er: J18erum higt euch, ich bete für euch!

Wenn Bekannte oder Verwandte keine lange Lebensdauer mehr vor sich hatten, konnte er dies immer, auf den Monat genau, mit voller Bestimmtheit sagen. Er kannte auch die Art des Todes und es stimmte jedesmal.

Wie mir Frau Zich mitteilte, handelte es sich bei den Briefen, die sie zu übersetzen hatte, meist um Fragen, welche den Zustand gewisser Verstorbener betraf.

Wenn an Pater Domenico eine Frage gestellt wurde, hielt er meist ein wenig inne, so, als ob er in Kontakt mit der Jbenc treten würde, was sicher auch der Fall gewesen ist, und dann antwortete er mit voller Bestimmtheit.

Fast jeder Mensch muß nach seinem Hinscheiden eine Zeit der Läuterung und Reinigung durchmachen, der eine länger, der andere kürzer, je nachdem es sein Seelenzustand erfordert.

Die Seele bleibt nach ihrem Hinscheiden noch eine zeitlang mit der örtlichen Umgebung, wo sie gelebt hat, verbunden. Es darf daher die Hinterbliebenen nicht verwundern, wenn sie in dieser Zeit manchmal seltsame Geräusche etc. wahrnehmen. das sei ganz normal. Sie sollen aber mit dem Medium hier einschalten wollen, mit dem Wunsch, mit dem Heimgegangenen in Kontakt zu kommen. Die Seele des oder der Heimgegangenen befindet sich jetzt in einer anderen Dimension. Man solle für sie beten und das Meßopfer darbringen lassen. Nur so kann man ihnen helfen.

Pater Domenico sagte von sich. er sei kein 1Hellseher, im üblichen Sinn, sondern er wird vom Heiligen Geist inspiriert. Pater Domenico sah sich selber immer nur als «armer Pater».

Er war für alle da, die zu ihm kamen, ohne Unterschied der Person, des Ranges oder Standes. Sein Tagewerk war sehr anstrengend. Oft wurde er an die siebzig Male von seiner Zelle heruntergeholt und mußte ebenso viele Male die Stufen zum Gnadenbild des hist. Antlitzes hinaufsteigen. um mit den Pilgergruppen zu beten und ihnen das wunderbare Vorkommnis zu erklären. Dazu kam noch die persönliche Aussprache mit den Einzelnen.

Völlig als Pilger, welche zum hist. Antlitz pilgerten, wollten auch mit Pater Domenico sprechen. Dadurch fühlten sich manche seiner Mitbruder im Kloster zurückgesetzt und waren Pater Domenico aus Neid und Eifersucht mißgünstig, was ihm das Leben im Kloster oft sehr schwer machte. Pater Domenico ertrug das alles mit Sanftmut und Geduld. Zur wahren Vollkommenheit gelangt man eben nur auf dem Weg des Kreuzes. Zudem ward P. Domenico durch seine Begnadung ein gar großes Apostolat aufgetragen. Ein Apostolat kann aber nur fruchtbar werden durch Mühsal, Opfer, Verkennung und Verfolgung und wie an die vielen Kreuze und Leiden heißen, die einem Menschen begegnen können. Das Einwirken der Gnade Gones und das Mitwirken des Menschen verhält sich im Vergleich so ähnlich wie das Gedeihen und Reiten der Früchte. Der Mensch ist gleichsam der Ackerboden. Dieser muß gepflügt, geeggt, immer wieder umgeackert und betreut werden. In diesem Ackerboden legt Gou den guten Samen und die verschiedenen Talente. Er sendet Sonnenschein und Regen, Wind und Gewitter, damit der Same sich entfalten kann. Der Acker kann sich nur zur Verfügung stellen und muß wohlwollend alles ertragen, was dem Gedeihen des Semens förderlich ist, um Frucht zu bringen. Ist es nicht so?

Nun aber wieder zu Pater Domenico. An manchen Tagen kamen drei bis vier Pilgergruppen zu Pater Domenico. Jede, einzelne wollte mit ihm sprechen. Ihm seine Anliegen vortragen usw. Das bedeutete für ihn eine ganz große physische und psychische Anstrengung für Pater Domenico, die so verschiedenartigen Probleme der einzelnen zu konzentrieren. Pater Domenico war wie mit dem ersten. so auch mit dem letzten Besucher gleich gut, gleich freundlich mit seiner ganzen Aufmerksamkeit. Man muß aber bedenken, daß er, wenn sich Pilgergruppen angemeldet hatten, vorher, ganze Nächte durchwacht und durchbetet hatte.

Am Abend waren seine Füße oft so stark angeschwollen, daß sie nach Beendigung eines langen Tagewerkes den todmüten Pater fast nicht mehr tragen konnten. Er aber wies keinen ab, sondern harrte aus bis zum Schluß und immer milder gleichen Güte. Das will etwas heißen!

Begreiflich. daß viele bei Pater Domenico die hl. Beichte ablegen wollten, andere wieder fuhren oft von weit her, um sich von Pater Domenico trauen oder ihr Kind taufen zu lassen. Er war auch vielen Priestern ein Ratgeber! Sein Ruf drang weit über die Grenzen hinaus. Seine Beliebtheit und Popularität steigerte sich, aber auch der Neid und die Mißgunst manches Mitbruders, der auch von der Vollkommenheit noch ein großes Stück entfernt war. Und so war man bestrebt, es bei den Oberen zu erreichen, daß Pater Domenico versetzt werde. Der liebe Gott aber ließ es nicht so weit kommen. Er sagte in Seinem ewigen Ratschluß: «Jetzt ist es genuglc Er holte ganz unerwartet den guten Pater Domenico zu sich ins Paradies. Doch davon splitter.

Fortsetzung folgt

◆◆◆◆◆◆◆◆◆◆◆◆◆◆◆◆◆◆◆◆◆◆◆◆◆◆

Da Stockschneida Anderl
hat oft was vabrocha,
drum is er scho xmal
6n Arrest einikrocha.

Ganz ausnahmsweis is er
heut' wi'eda amol frei.
Sein erster Weg führt'n
6s Wirtshiusl nei.

Da trinkt er so vie'
und so Jang a's er kann.
Fallt draußt au! das Straß
und kimmt akkrat dort an,

wo drunt da städtische Kanai vobeirinnt.
Er 20gt 20 aufs Gads und gleich schafft er ein,
'Ma er munta w,fd, denkt er:
wo wü,l i denn sein?

Da hebt er an Kopf, s18cht's Gada und schreit:
"JWegn was bi i hiatzt denn scho wieda so weit?ttr

◆◆◆◆◆◆◆◆◆◆◆◆◆◆◆◆◆◆◆◆◆◆◆◆◆◆

Kaiser Karl von Österreich

(Fortsetzung.)

Eine der hervorstechendsten Eigenschaften des Dieners Gones Karl aus dem Hause Österreich war, daß er in seinem Mitmenschen immer nur das Gute gesehen und stets an das Gute im Menschen geglaubt hat, auch wenn er oft Böses erfahren mußte. Es war ihm ganz einfach unmöglich zu glauben, daß jemand bewußt etwas Böses macht, da für ihn jeder Mensch das hervorragendste Abbild Gones war.

Diesen Charakterzug des späteren Dieners Gones finden wir bereits beim jungen Erzherzog, aus dessen Leben uns folgendes erzählt wird:

In der frühesten Jugendzeit erlitt Erzherzog Karl einen Unfall, der ihn für immer die volle Beweglichkeit des linken Fußes kostete. Es war im Winter und er war mit seinem Erzieher zum Eislaufplatz gegangen. Beim Gehen auf dem Eise. was er mit großer Freude tat, begegnete ihm ein junge, Mann, der ungefähr seines Alters war und dr' sich einen boshaften Scherz daraus machen wollte, den Erzherzog niederzuwerfen. Schon war es dem Erzherzog gelungen. ihm einmal auszuweichen.

Das nächste Mal aber kam der junge Mann von rückwärts, fing mit seinem Schlittschuh den hinteren Teil des Schlittschuhes Erzherzog Karts, schwang sich nach vorne herum und lief, sich rasch loslösend, weg. Diese Bewegung drehte den linken Fuß des Erzherzogs vollständig nach rückwärts und der Loslösungsdruck war so heftig. daß Erzherzog Karl das Gleichgewicht verlor und sich mit Gewalt auf das umgedrehte Bein setzte. Ein dreimaliger spiralförmiger Bruch des Schienbeines und des Fußansatzes waren die Folge davon. Der Erzieher eilte erschrocken herbei und der junge Mann, der den Unfall verursacht hatte, stürzte ebenfalls mit anderen Zuschauern zurück und gab sich den Anschein, als ob er gar nicht in der Nähe gewesen wäre und nun zu Hilfe herbeieilte. Der jugendliche Erzherzog schwieg in seinen furchtbaren Schmerzen und erzählte mit keinem Wort, welche Rolle der angebliche Helfer in Wirklichkeit gespielt hatte. Es wurde daher vermutet, daß er einfach ausgeglitten und ungeschickt hingefallen wäre. Diese Auslegung wurde dann allerdings durch den Arzt zunichte gemacht. der eine Drehung von ungeheurer Vehemenz konstatierte. Indem der junge Erzherzog seine Schmerzen energisch verbiß. wurden die Knochen ohne Narkose gefugt und nach den ersten zwei bis drei Wochen wußte man noch nicht, ob Überhaupt eine Verheilung stattfinden würde.

Durch Kombination kam Graf Wallis auf den Grund der Geschichte. Er erfuhr nämlich. daß am gleichen Tage auf dem Eislaufplau mehrere Leute durch einen

97

98

"Grüß Gott!", Jg. 5, 1982, Heft 9+10, S.97 + 98

When her marriage was approaching, Mrs. Wimmer begged the Prelate Holböck to ask Padre Domenico if the boyfriend was the right person for her.

Padre Domenico said many things but the German priest did not translate a single word. Just a year after the wedding, her husband died. Mrs. Wimmer was convinced that Padre Domenico predicted the premature death of her husband and that the Prelate Holböck did not want to tell her anything.

Elisabeth Wimmer from Salzburg (on the left pictured with her brother-in-law) was the tailor of Ida Loidl.

Thanks to her, this writer has been able to obtain many issues of the magazine "Grüß Gott!": She told me that, for Ida Loidl, Padre Domenico was a great saint.

Ida Loidl died suddenly, October 22, 1985, just as she was about to print the November-December 1985 issue of "Grüß Gott!"

May the blessing of Padre Domenico accompany her!

The fame of Padre Domenico grew ever further and further, so that the number of pilgrims from the Germanic area also increased.

With them he sang the Christmas song, "Silent Night" and especially with all his heart, "Christ, the Savior is here."

(Photos of groups from Germany: Palatinate and Augsburg).

Since the mid-seventies Padre Domenico wanted to learn to drive. As Fra Vincenzo recounted, it was enough for him to read the handbooks only once to pass the theory test. From July 15, 1975 he was enrolled in the Autoclub Pescara. The July 17, 1976 he received the license plate for his car. But he had difficulty with the practical part of driving. Thank goodness that his guardian angels protected him!

With the car, he wanted to save time and reach people in Manoppello and Lettomanoppello, to give them the anointing of the sick and the last comfort.

Fra Vincenzo recounts while smiling: *"Sometimes I ran after him saying "do not forget to turn off the lights when you get out of the car, otherwise the battery will be down" ... or "pay attention to the trees, when you park!"*

The first car accident happened on October 26, 1976; he was not guilty but the car was wrecked and he was hospitalized. (on the left the accident report, signed by Padre Domenico)

On January 26, 1977 Padre Domenico bought a new car, a Fiat 126; he was again ready to bring the Lord to the needy. But after a year and a half – in August of 1978 – the second accident did happen. Once again, it was not his fault but the damages were greater this time.

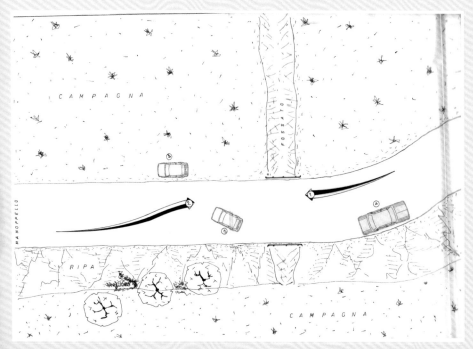

There were three cars involved in the accident: a driver from Rome had turned at full speed at the corner on the Via Vallone in Manoppello losing control of the vehicle (on the left a sketch of the accident).

It was not due to be the last accident in the life of Padre Domenico!

The major religious event of 1978 was the exhibition of the Turin Shroud. After 45 years, it was exhibited again, in the cathedral from August 26 to October 8, 1978. The occasion was the four hundredth anniversary of the transfer of the Shroud from Chambery (France) to Turin. Crowds of people wanted to see and worship the burial cloth; one of them was Padre Domenico da Cese.

Tuesday, September 12, 1978, the day of the Feast of the Most Holy Name of Mary, Padre Domenico's greatest wish was fulfilled. Together with his friends, Sante Burchi, who had often gone with him to Lourdes, Agostina Lazzarini and Mr. Francesco Chionni from Rieti, he could finally drive to Turin to see the Holy Shroud. It was as if the name of Mary had opened the doors to allow him to finally see the Face of Our Lord Jesus Christ when he was dead, while he saw the Face of the Risen One every day.

Around 8 p.m., it was already dark, Francesco Chionni pressed the gas-pedal to get to Turin faster. Padre Domenico said: "With this speed we could reach the eternal happiness and to truth first!"

Wednesday September 13 was the anniversary of Fatima: 60 years earlier, Our Lady appeared to the three young shepherds in the Cova da Iria in Portugal. She had always guided Padre Domenico on the way of the Lord.

Early in the morning he celebrated Mass for his small group of pilgrims in the church St. Theresa of the Child Jesus (A, see map).

What a timely coincidence! Sr. Theresa of the Child Jesus (1873-1897) had chosen to add "and of the Holy Face" to her title.

In 1898, a year after Theresa's death, Secondo Pia took the famous photo of the Shroud, which started new and deep researches and spread its cult.

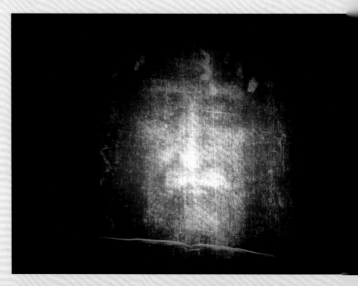

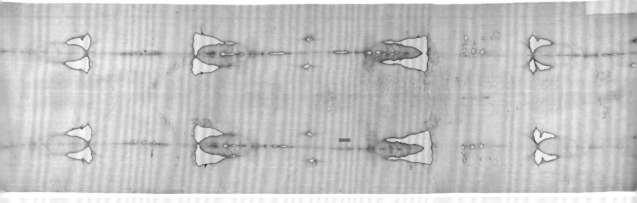

At 11 a.m., after a long wait spent in prayer in the Cathedral of Turin, they finally reached the Holy Shroud (B). Only a short time they could stay in front of it. Few precious moments, to thank the Lord for opening to us, with the Redemption, the path to heaven. Padre Domenico's eyes searched intensely for the Face of Jesus. Francesco Chionni recounts what happened later:

At 6 p.m., Padre Domenico celebrated again in the Church of Mary Help of Christians (C). Then everyone went to my aunt's house who lived in Via Paolo Braccini, 29 (D).

We arrived around 8:40 p.m. Padre Domenico was about to cross the road, which was completely free. Everything was quiet, there was no traffic. I was a few yards behind him and I was carrying his bag. Suddenly, a Fiat 500 came at full speed and hitting directly the father, who was about 1 yard from the sidewalk, knocking him to the ground.

He fell like Jesus under the cross; he was bleeding from the nose and from the wounds on his head. We thought he was dead on the spot. I shouted: "Padre Pio, save him! Madonna, save him!" I lifted his head, held it in my hands, and heard him murmur, "What a blow! It could only be me!"

The map on the right shows the path that Padre Domenico made that day in Turin.

The points marked with different colors indicate his pilgrimage and highlight it on the map.

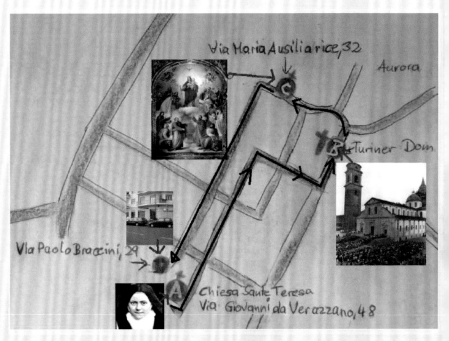

The site of the accident in 1978 (left) and how it looks today.

Both the police and the ambulance arrived immediately. Padre Domenico was taken to the "Mauriziano," the nearest hospital. Since there were no free beds and he had severe pains in the chest and shoulder, he was transported to the Main Hospital "Molinette." The diagnosis: fracture of the ribs. The same night Fr. Pietro was sent from Manoppello to stay close to Padre Domenico; the Brother arrived in Turin the following morning.

On Thursday, September 14, Padre Domenico had severe pains all day long that prevented him from speaking. Sante Burchi, who slept in the same room, heard him talking in his sleep, as if he were confessing people and then absolving them. But it did not seem to him that Padre Domenico was delirious.

Don Aldo Bollini visited Padre Domenico in the hospital together with A. Ruffini, who had the stigmata as Padre Pio. Here they are both in the picture on the left.

Every day also Giovanni Cardelli visited him. He was the young motorist who caused the accident and was inconsolable about it.

Father Pietro recalled how Padre Domenico, though presenting a large hematoma on his back, was cheerful in his bed; he thought then that it was only a matter of time and that Padre Domenico would recover completely.

On Saturday, September 16, at 6:55 a.m., Padre Domenico said: *"...it is an offer for the Shroud of Turin."* At about 1:55 p.m., he was heard to say to himself: *".... universal joy: the Church of God."*

Agostina Lazzarini later reported that Padre Domenico in those days had talked a lot about the Holy Face and its diffusion, for example, of the *"theological value of the proclamation of the death and the resurrection."*

And he taught this prayer:

"Eternal Father,

We offer you the Face

of your beloved Son,

worthy of being worshiped,

in honor of Your holy name,

for the triumph of the Church,

for the salvation of Italy and

of the whole world."

In this connection, he finally concluded to Agostina:

"What you do not understand now, you will understand it in the hour of the trial!"

Sunday September 17 was the day of the Feast of the Exaltation of the Holy Cross and the Impression of the Stigmata of St. Francis.

Let us listen again to Francesco Chionni: In the morning at 5 a.m., Padre Domenico said:

"Take and eat, this is my body ...

Take and drink, this is my blood ...

Bring everything to the Eucharist!

Receive Holy Communion!

Venerate the Holy Face! I will stay close to you and grant you many graces."

Other words spoken on that day by Padre Domenico:

"Angel of God, you are my guardian, enlighten, guard, hold and govern me, that I was entrusted to you by the heavenly compassion. Amen!"

"Now let us entrust ourselves to the mercy of the Lord, who sustains us, and to the help of Saint Joseph."

"Be good, be strong! – and you will always do well."

"The Lord sees you, blesses you and makes his Face shine on you, the Lord Jesus, who is mercy, gives you peace, may the Lord Jesus give you his blessing and free you from all evil." In the name of the Father and Son and of the Holy Spirit, Amen."

Giovanni Cardelli, who had caused the accident, came again with his girlfriend. Padre Domenico blessed the young man and said to him: *"I do not mind, you know, I am old and if I die, it does not matter, but you are young, live well, with faith in God, and prepare well for marriage."*

A nun also came who wanted spiritual advice from him. He gave her the answer, marked by great wisdom, and she went away moved and reassured.

Even the chaplain, the nurses and the doctors were impressed by his wisdom and depth.

It was around 9:30 p.m., when his spiritual daughter Amalia Di Rella arrived from Bari together with the Del Vecchio family.

At about 10:30 p.m. Padre Domenico slightly opened his left eye; he hardly breathed, gave one last glance to his spiritual family, and then closed his eyes in silence. He died very peacefully and without further movement.

The photo on the right shows Padre Domenico just after his death.

On his body friends placed a prayer leaflet of the Holy Face and a rose.

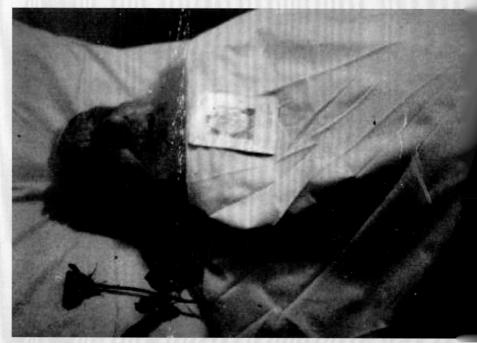

While Padre Domenico was dying at the hospital in Turin, the well-known writer Renzo Allegri (1934, pictured left) arrived in Manoppello. In 1963, he was the first to publish a book on Pope John XXIII (then still alive) that had made him famous.

In September 1978, Allegri then went to Manoppello to have Padre Domenico reveal the secret of the Holy Face. Since the Father was not in a convent, the guardian, Father Luciano Antonelli, gave him the interview; later he reported that he had only said what he had learned from Padre Domenico. The article was published in the popular magazine 'GENTE' and was the beginning of the spread of the Holy Face.

The article by Renzo Allegri was read by Paul Otto Schenker, the founder of the "Immaculate Editions" in Switzerland, who was so impressed that he translated the text into German and published it in the "Zeichen Mariens" edition published in November 1978. Thus, the fame of the Holy Face spread more and more in the German-speaking countries.

Even earlier there had been, in Germany, those who had recognized the importance of the Holy Face. -In the last part of the article (on the right) Herbert Mayrhofer, a Brother of the Sacred Heart, when comparing the image of Manoppello's face with that of Turin, came to the conclusion that the two faces belong to the same person: Jesus Christ!

DAS "VOLTO SANTO" VON MANOPPELLO

Post Scriptum:

On June 5, 1976, Fr. Herbert Mayfhofer, MSC, Arnsberg, already known to our readers for the stories of pilgrimages, wrote to us among other things:

«...With joy and great interest, I had followed your initiative for the Holy Face of the Shroud that must have left in those who have seen it closely, a very profound impression. In Turin, we have before us the image of Our Lord as a dead man; but there is another Face in which the Risen Savior looks at us, with a depth and transparency that do not strike less: his gaze deeply disturbs our soul. This Holy Face is unfortunately sonly slightly known.

On May 3, 1976, I was with a group of pilgrims in Manoppello where the sudarium of Jesus is kept. During the celebration of Holy Mass, after the consecration, the curtain on the tabernacle was pulled from one side and we could see the Holy Face of Our Lord. The impression was enormous. One might think that the Risen One is in our midst and says: "Do not be afraid. It's me. Peace be with you! ».

Later I had the opportunity to compare the Face of Manoppello with the Face of the Holy Shroud of Turin and I found obvious coincidences, which catch the eye. Not only in the many scars but also in the folds of the fabric, in the swelling of the face and in other points. To tell the truth, once we have before us the somewhat emaciated face of Our dead Lord, which, as happens for the dead, appears to us a little different and gives us a certain impression, while the face of a living person radiates strength and real presence. This also happens here. But precisely this gives us the certainty that what we have before us, in both cases, is the authentic face of Jesus Christ ....

Br. H. Mayrhofer msc

The death of Padre Domenico was like a key that opened the door to the recognition and diffusion of the Holy Face. The article published in the journal, "Zeichen Mariens" attracted the attention of Sister Blandina Schlömer, OCSO and then of Fr. Heinrich Pfeiffer S.J. as well of Paul Badde..

Fr. Pietro was sent to Turin to assist Padre Domenico and was hosted in the convent of the Capuchins. What was his amazement in meeting two fathers of his religious province, both there to see the Shroud. When they heard that Padre Domenico had a car accident and died, one of the two, Fr. Cristofaro Foschini, did not think twice and went immediately to the coffin to read the office of the dead.

On the right picture below, the wound on the head that Padre Domenico had acquired in the accident is well visible.

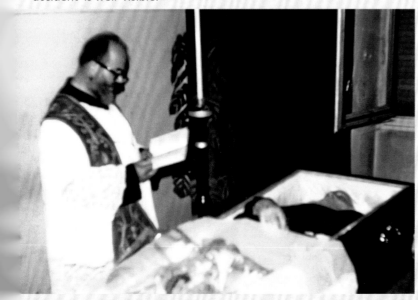
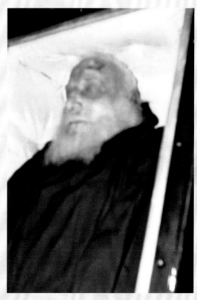

Father Pietro reported that Padre Domenico was transported with a hearse from Turin to Manoppello. From the picture we learned that the transport took place on September 19, 1978.

FRATERNITA' CAPPUCCINA SANTUARIO DEL VOLTO SANTO · MANOPPELLO.

Vittima di un incidente della strada, avvenuto in Torino nel corso di un pellegrinaggio alla S. Sindone, è tragicamente scomparso il

R.P. Domenico Petracca da Cese

La Fraternità Cappuccina di Manoppello, nel darne l'annunzio ai fedeli che tanto l'amavano, ricorda ed esalta le sue nobili virtù di sacerdote e di religioso.

La sua fedeltà incrollabile alla Chiesa e all'Ordine, la sua purezza di mente e di cuore, il suo insegnamento generoso ed efficace restano per tutti noi un esempio da imitare.

Dalla Misericordia Divina imploriamo per la Sua anima eletta la pace dei giusti.

Le esequie avranno luogo presso questo Santuario il giorno 20 alle ore 16

" Gloriosa è la morte che paga col sangue una vita immortale "

Impresa Pompe Funebri CREMONESE & Figli Manoppello

On September 20, 1978, it was a Wednesday, the solemn funeral Mass was held at 4:00 p.m. in the Sanctuary of the Holy Face in Manoppello.

The obituary was posted everywhere, on the trees and wherever there was a free place.

Sister Amalia and her friends attended the wake until the church was open to the public, and the many people waiting, entered for the funeral Mass. The images speak for themselves.

To the right we see Sister Amalia Di Rella (wearing a white cap) during the wake.

Below on the left: It almost seems as if Padre Domenico wants to look at his beloved, even when he's dead, with his half-open left eye.

Below on the right: Fr. Lucine Antonelli, at that time Rector of the Sanctuary (left) and Fr. Vincenzo d'Elpidio (right), very close to Padre Domenico.

At the funeral Mass about 60 priests participated and a huge crowd gathered from all over Italy. It was officiated by the Bishop of Chieti-Vasto, the future Cardinal Vincenzo Fagiolo (1918-2000), pictured on the right.

After the funeral Mass in Manoppello, Padre Domenico was transported to Cese to find his last resting place in the village where he was born. As Padre Domenico had often talked about erecting a chapel, the relatives thought he wanted to be buried in a larger space where a Mass could be celebrated.

In the picture above, the inhabitants of Cese gave him the last farewells in the church of the village.

Here Padre Domenico rested until the family tomb was finished.

Above we see the photo of the tomb of the Petracca family where Padre Domenico is currently resting.

In the photo on the right, the epigraph written on the tombstone of Padre Domenico that testifies to the veneration he still enjoys among the faithful.

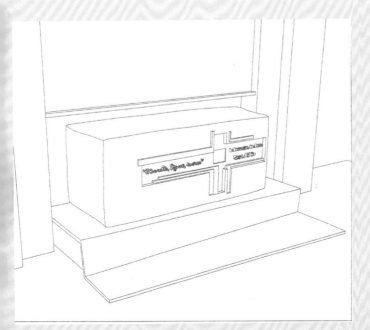

Many faithful rejoice that the mortal remains of Padre Domenico will be brought back to Manoppello.

The new tomb is being prepared in the Sanctuary of the Holy Face. In the picture on the left you see a sketch of the project.

Many people reported that Padre Domenico da Cese had Jesus' stigmata. But there were others who said: "No, he did not have them" or "I did not see them."

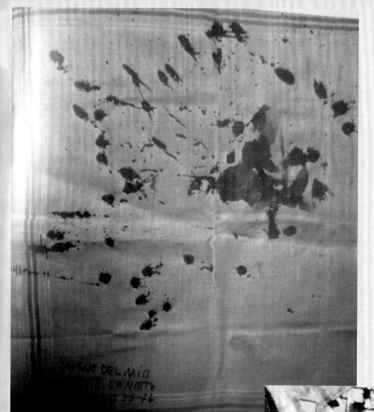

On a handkerchief Padre Domenico wrote with his own blood: ***"Blood from my side, in the night of March 3, 1976."*** It is a testimony of having taken upon himself the sufferings of Christ.

Perhaps he had been chosen to carry on himself, in a hidden form, the sufferings of His Lord, if this was the will of the Father.

Seeing these photos, everyone can get their own idea, whether or not Padre Domenico had the stigmata.

On the right we see another handkerchief stained with the blood of Padre Domenico (1976)

On the left: This picture was taken during his trip to Israel in 1967.

On the right: the enlargement shows the closed wounds.

Unfortunately, an undated photo:

The wound is well visible.

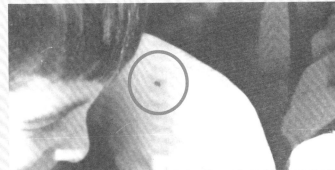

Manoppello, undated.

Above: the wound is open, while
at the bottom it is closed.

During a Mass in Campli, undated.

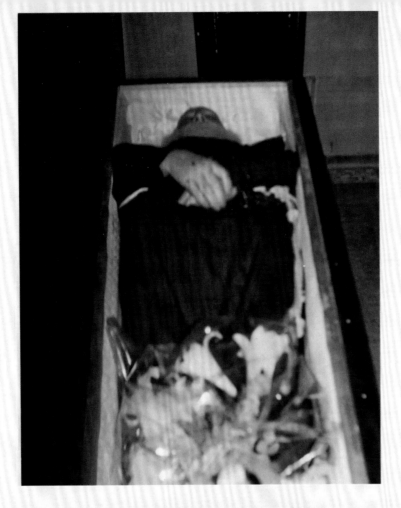

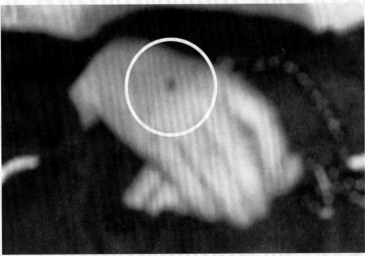

Turin: The wound on the right hand is open.

The photos suggest that Padre Domenico da Cese, like Saint Catherine of Siena or Theresa Neumann from Konnersreuth had the stigmata, but they appeared only on certain occasions. The pain was present, but the wounds were not visible.

Perhaps this explains what Padre Domenico once told Maria Venditti: *"I cannot work with my own hands, because I always have pain."*

Padre Domenico, pray for us!